Diamondola
&
Aram

Middle East Ambassadors

By
Mildred Thompson Olson

TEACH Services, Inc.
P U B L I S H I N G
www.TEACHServices.com

———————————————

Copyright © 2004 TEACH Services, Inc.
ISBN-13: 978-1-578258-279-8
Library of Congress Control Number: 2004105705

Published by

TEACH Services, Inc.
P U B L I S H I N G
www.TEACHServices.com

DEDICATION

To Diamondola and Aram's daughter, Indra, her husband, Lee Greer, and Ashods' grandchildren, Lee III and Ruth, I dedicate this book. Diamondola's diary facilitated me in writing these pages. I am indebted to her and Indra for editing my manuscript. With solemn admiration I would also acknowledge the Adventist Christians, both living and dead, who endured courageously the years of persecution in Turkey from approximately 1900 to 1923.

SPECIAL NOTATION

Diamondola's life touched a multitude of people. Due to sensitive situations that may still exist for some of her friends, I have sometimes used pseudonyms to protect their privacy.

I would also caution the reader to distinguish clearly between the government of Turkey in those days of suspicion before 1930 and the government of today. Please do not assume that the political climate and government in modern Turkey is the same as it was in Ashods' days. As America has made progress/changes through the years, so has the rest of the world. Furthermore, the Moslems in the Middle East are usually friends to Seventh-day Adventists. We share some common beliefs in regard to health and idol worship. There are a few fanatics in every society who tend to make a bad name for their people/country. Unfortunately, it is that kind of person who is sometimes in power. Please bear that thought in mind as you read this book and form a charitable opinion of the people of the Middle East.

Other books by
Mildred Thompson Olson

The Making of Midge
Midge on Her Own
Midge in Lebanon
Diamondola
Midge & Wayne in the Middle East

CONTENTS

INTRODUCTION

For those who have not read my book DIAMONDOLA, this brief summary of it will help the reader better understand DIAMONDOLA AND ARAM.

Diamondola was born March 24, 1894, to Theodora and Elijah Keanides. Her parents were Greeks living in Eskishehir, Turkey, a town almost 150 miles west of Ankara. She was a very frail child physically, but God gave her an exceedingly brilliant mind. When she was only a few months old, she was baptized into the Greek Orthodox Church. Soon after that, some relatives, including her father Elijah and sisters Alexandra (15) and Susanna (13), became Protestants. Religious prejudices ostracized them from the community. They moved to Brousa, a town 100 miles southeast of Constantinople (called Istanbul today). There the family became Seventh-day Adventists which complicated their lives still further.

Mr. Keanides was imprisoned for possessing Adventist literature. After his release, he became an invalid. The family was destitute so mother Theodora set up silk-weaving looms in their house. Diamondola educated herself at home while weaving silk cloth, her textbooks propped up beside her loom. Beside the regular school subjects, Diamondola mastered the Armenian, Greek, Turkish, and English languages through self-taught grammar books.

The church utilized Diamondola's gift for languages when she was only 13. Elder AcMoody made an extended missionary journey throughout Turkey using little Diamondola as his translator. Three years later (1910) she spent several months translating for Elder Greaves in Greece and Albania.

Diamondola had only three years of formal education when she graduated from the American High School in Brousa in 1912. That summer the Levant Mission in Constantinople hired her as the translator and secretary. She improved her evenings by learning French and German, making a total of six languages in which she was now fluent.

When her father died in 1913, Diamondola moved her mother to Constantinople where she could care for her. At the mission, Diamondola met and became engaged to Ares, a young minister. The next year the mission sent him to preach in Greece where he died in 1916 of tuberculosis.

In the meantime, Diamondola was arrested for sending out "propaganda". The Adventist literature (propaganda) Diamondola had sent throughout Turkey contained Biblical references to Christ's second coming—which had absolutely nothing to do with World War I nor the political situation. Diamondola was imprisoned and forced to represent herself before the judgment bar of Bedri Bey, the cruel chief of security in war-time Turkey. With the Bible in her hand and an angel by her side, Diamondola bore witness for her faith in Jesus. In the hushed courtroom, many were "almost persuaded" to believe in Jesus. Bedri Bey set Diamondola free.

Diamondola made her third missionary journey throughout Turkey with Elder Frauchiger during the winter of 1915–16. Their purpose was to ease the suffering of the Christians being deported by the Turkish government. They brought food, clothing, and money to the deportees on their death march into Syria. Most of the Adventists, along with a million other Christians, perished in the genocide.

INTRODUCTION

In 1919, Diamondola was made secretary-treasurer for the Levant Union Mission, a very heavy responsibility for a 25 year old. With the ministers and colporteurs either dead, deported, or imprisoned, the Erzburgers and Diamondola were swamped with work. During the reconstruction period following the war, Christian refugees started pouring back into Constantinople. At the mission, Erzburgers, Diamondola, and her mother, Theodora, worked around the clock caring for the pitiful wrecks of humanity who fell at their doorstep. Their spirits needing to be rekindled, and their bodies needing to be revitalized. One young mother, infested with typhus, died in Diamondola's arms. A few weeks later Diamondola, weak from exhaustion and over-exposure, came down with the disease and died. With intense sorrow Mrs. Erzburger and Diamondola's mother prepared her body for burial. Six hours later, Elder Tcharakian arrived. He looked down upon the still, stiff form of God's little warrior and realized that the mission had no one to replace her. Like Peter in the case of Dorcas, he knelt with the two ladies and prayed "… in the name of Jesus, I say unto you arise." He was not surprised when God rewarded his faith by resurrecting Diamondola.

By 1920, refugees coming from the interior of Turkey with no money and no place to go, over-ran the mission offices. The mission workers did not feel that they could push the pathetic refugees into the street so they gave them temporary shelter inside the mission offices. But the mission work suffered. To provide a sanctuary for everyone, the mission rented Rumeli Hissar, a huge rambling house with a garden on the outskirts of Constantinople. Here the whole mission staff lived together with the orphans and refugees until papers for their emigration could be processed.

Fortunately, Elder and Mrs. Buzugherian, who had fled to Egypt during the war, returned to Constantinople and relieved the Erzburgers and Diamondola from some of the mission work. With the Erzburgers came Aram Ashod, an Armenian soldier in the Turkish army who had been captured and held as a prisoner of war for three years by the British army. He also joined the mission staff. The extra help at the mission freed the Erzburgers and Diamondola to attend the Seventh-day Adventist European Conference in Zurich, Switzerland.

Aram fell in love with Diamondola when he first saw her in 1915, but she was engaged to Ares at the time. Now that Ares was gone, Aram pursued his interest in Diamondola. This did not escape the notice of the Rumeli Hissar household. When she returned from Europe, there seemed to be a conspiracy among them to get Diamondola interested in Aram. Was it working? The book takes over from here.

The Author

Chapter One

ARAM'S DILEMMA

"Aram loves Diamondola. Aram loves Diamondola," chanted the young lad as he ducked behind the garden shed.

"Oh, be quiet, Manoug, and come out here where I can see you," Aram scolded as he dropped himself tiredly onto the white, wrought-iron bench.

"You ain't mad at me, are you?" Manoug asked anxiously as he crept from behind the shed, weaving his way through the hollyhocks toward Aram.

"No, I guess not, 'cause it's true. I do love Diamondola. The trouble is I'm not sure she loves me."

Manoug stood respectfully in front of Aram, like the dutiful servant his Syrian owners had trained to be. "But she should. All us orphan kids here at Rumeli Hissar like you Mr. Aram, Sir. You are like a papa to us."

"Manoug, will you stop calling me 'sir'? You are no longer the little slave boy in a Moslem Syrian home. You are among your Seventh-day Adventist Christian friends now. And as soon as your papers are processed, I will send you off on a big ship to America where you will be adopted by an Armenian family as their son. I've already found homes for some of the orphans who've passed through here since the Great War ended."

"I know you have, Sir, ah, I mean, Mr. Aram. But you know, us kids are kinda scared to leave here and go alone to someone

1

we've never seen. We feel safe here. I just want to live here forever with you and Miss Diamondola as my papa and mama."

"Come here, Manoug," Aram said tenderly as he took Manoug's hand and pulled him down onto the bench beside him. Aram put his arm around the lad's shoulders and tried to snuggle him close, but the boy sat rigid. "You aren't used to being hugged, are you, Manoug?"

"No, Sir. I used to see my Syrian master huggin' his little boy, but no one ever hugged me."

"Not even when you were a little boy with your papa and mama?"

"Yes. Well, I think I can remember sitting on mama's lap and bein' hugged and kissed. But I was only four then. Mama died, and the next year the Turkish soldiers took Papa, Joseph, and me into exile. That was in 1916. Papa and Joseph got sick and died along the way. Those mean soldiers just kicked their bodies off into the ditch. I screamed and cried 'cause I didn't want to leave them. The soldiers made fun of me and beat me. After that, I never felt nothin'. I was just sorta numb and wished I could die. But I didn't. Next I remember being taken to an auction in the public square of a big town. Men, women, boys, and girls were led one at a time up on a platform and sold to the Syrians. My master didn't know much Turkish and I knew no Arabic, so I was beaten quite a bit that first year because I didn't understand him."

"Did he give you good food to eat?" Aram asked solicitously.

"I ate what was left in the bottom of the kettles. It was enough"

"Where did you sleep, Manoug?"

"Oh, he made a lean-to on the side of the house, and I rolled up in a blanket and slept there. That's where the Red Cross ladies found me. My master tried to hide me because he didn't want to give up his slave, but I slipped away from him, ran to the ladies, and asked them to save me. They took me and brought me here. Now I don't want to remember anymore of those bad days."

Manoug's face looked drawn and old for his 10 years. Clearly he was trying to block from his memory his miserable past.

"I don't blame you," Aram sympathized. "I spent three of those war years down in Egypt as a prisoner of war, but the English treated us quite well. I was better off than the Armenians, like your parents, who remained in Turkey. But none of us had any choice. We were sent where the Turkish government wanted us. For the moment we Christians have a respite here in Turkey, but I don't think it will last. That's why I have to get as many of you refugees as possible to America where you'll be safe. And don't worry; your new parents will love you. Since your family died, you've lost the feeling of love. You have been scarred because you lacked love. I hope the feeling will come back to you. Then you'll be able to enjoy that contented feeling of being special, very special to some one. But I'm warning you, you'll have to let them hug and kiss you. That's what love is all about—caring, feeling, hugging, kissing, and touching."

"Would you hug and kiss Miss Diamondola?" Manoug asked, scandalized at the very thought. He leaned back and looked intently into Aram's face.

"Now look here, young man, don't you ask such personal questions!" It was Aram's turn for consternation. In 1920 men and women did not show affection in public, especially in the Middle East. No one told secrets of what went on in private, either. The 10-year old Manoug and 36-year old Aram were at an impasse. Neither spoke for a time.

Aram considered the boy's love-deprived background and thought he should talk like a papa to Manoug.

"Yes, Manoug, I would love to hug and kiss Miss Diamondola. And I will if she will become my wife. The Bible says that husbands are to love their wives."

"Oh, my goodness! Oh, no!" Manoug jumped to his feet and walked about clutching his stomach. "Oh, I never thought a MAN would kiss a WOMAN!"

"Well, they do. Mostly in private. And I hope the day will soon come when I can sneak Miss Diamondola away from the rest of this household and kiss her."

Manoug was still repulsed by the thought of such intimacy. "Well, if that's what you want, you'd better ask Miss Diamondola to marry you soon."

"That's exactly what I intend to do. I came out here into the garden this evening to plan my strategy."

"But you have all kinds of chances to ask her. You ride the ferry and tram to and from work with her every day. You work all day at the office with her. You live right here at Rumeli Hissar, the mission communal house, with her! What's the matter with you guys?"

"Well, now it isn't as easy as you think," Aram found himself stammering for a logical explanation. "Women like to be, well, to feel courted."

"Courted? What do you mean by that?"

"Courting a lady means you take her places, do special things for her, buy her candy or other nice things."

"Okay. So do it! All the people here in the commune say you love Diamondola, and we don't want to be shipped out until we see you married."

"Is that so? Well, I'll have to do something about that real…"

"Aram, where are you?" Diamondola called as she came through the kitchen door carrying two pails. "It's time for us to go get the milk."

"I'm here, Miss Diamondola, and I'm ready," Aram called back with a lilt in his voice. He rose quickly from the bench, winked at Manoug, and joined Diamondola at the back gate of the garden. Going after milk from the neighbor had become an evening ritual for the two of them. It was the one time in the day when they could be away from the busy household in which they lived and the frustration of the office in which they worked. It was a time to relax together.

"Good luck, Mr. Aram, Sir," called a child's voice from the hollyhock patch.

"Good luck, Mr. Aram, Sir?" questioned Diamondola. "Whatever for?"

"Oh, I wish you knew," Aram mumbled. "You, ah, you could be my good luck. In the meantime, I'll just try to, to, ah, open the gate for you."

Diamondola was baffled by Aram's nervous behavior. It didn't improve on the way home, either. Suddenly Aram stopped, set down his pail of milk with a splash, and asked, "Miss Diamondola, when are we going to get married?"

"Oh, I don't know," she answered casually, walking on with her pail of milk.

"We'll have to think about it," she added without turning her head or slowing her pace.

Pursing his lips, Aram drew a deep breath, exhaled explosively, snatched up his pail of milk, and hastened his steps to keep stride with her. In his rush some of the milk sloshed over the bucket, spattering his polished black shoes. Had Aram been able to read her mind, he would have known that Diamondola's words and actions belied her inner feelings. Since he couldn't guess what she was thinking, he was baffled and wondered what to say next. He admitted to himself that he had not made the most romantic proposal—not even a diplomatic one. Just a blurted-out one. But there was a glimmer of hope. She hadn't outright refused his proposal, just stalled for time. Watching her intently from the corner of his eye, he stumbled along beside her and tried again. "When will you know, Diamondola?"

"After we've prayed about it," she answered evenly, never even glancing his way.

When they reached the back gate, Aram set down his pail with another splash. Blocking Diamondola's passage, he grasped her shoulders gently, and turned her toward him. "Look, little Darling, everyone expects us to get married. We know each other well, and we are in love, aren't we? Why wait longer?"

As Aram started to pull Diamondola into his arms, she deliberately placed her pail of milk between them and looked him in the eye. "Aram," she said, "do you mind if we pray about it a little more?"

Aram's hands dropped back to his sides; he leaned over and picked up what was left of his pail of milk. "As you say, Diamondola," he agreed reluctantly.

He was disappointed to the point of depression. Things had not gone as he had hoped. In the morning he'd have to tell Manoug, "No luck."

Aram could not realize how much he had shaken Diamondola. Upstairs in her room alone that night, Diamondola paced the floor, prayed to God, and reasoned with herself. She began to question her position on marriage. She loved Aram. Would it be wrong for her to marry him and enjoy a little domestic security and bliss? Or did God want her to devote full time and effort to His work as she had done since the age of 13. She had been engaged to Ares once, and that didn't seem wrong. When Ares died four years ago, she had put marriage out of her mind and heart. Now Aram's proposal threatened that resolve. He was kind and thoughtful, courting her gently and lovingly. She could hardly help but like him—yes, maybe she even loved him. Why should she not seek happiness with a devoted Christian worker such as he? He had been a tremendous blessing to the work ever since he had returned from Egypt. He had gradually taken over most of the actual publishing work for the union. He also helped Diamondola with the accounts. Now, when Diamondola had only translation work to do, she could stay home and do it in her room. She could concentrate better there and work faster than in the office. "Oh, what shall I do?" she asked herself as she dropped onto her bed exhausted.

As Diamondola tossed restlessly on her bed, she admitted that she had come to depend a great deal on Aram's help. She was drawn to him as a person, but she wanted a clear directive from God. What was His will for her? She finally drifted off to sleep believing that, as He had led her in the past, He would continue to guide her now.

The next morning she was too tired to rush off to the office with Aram. She stayed out of sight until he left. Then she dressed carefully for the day. As she combed her brown tresses up into a bun, she examined herself in the mirror. "How can Aram love anyone as skinny as me? He says I'm beautiful. MEN! That's what they all say." She turned to the paper she was translating from English into Turkish. "Let me get back to the real world—work!"

Early that afternoon as Diamondola was working on the manuscripts, she had an overpowering urge to walk over to the window and look out. She repressed the impulse several times, but finally she yielded and walked over to the window. As she looked down the path, she saw Aram coming up from the boat landing. She smiled and waved to him, and Aram returned the greeting.

Instinctively, Diamondola knew that what had just happened had special significance. Her heart was doing double time as Aram burst through the door.

He rushed over to her and lifted her into his arms. "Don't refuse any longer, my Dearest," he said, kissing her cheeks and lips. "I prayed about the matter, and my prayer was answered—you were standing at the window."

"I will marry you, Aram," Diamondola whispered in his ear as she hugged him tightly. "It feels so good to love and be loved again."

The next Sabbath, Aram and Diamondola invited everyone to attend their engagement party the following Sunday on the lawn of Rumeli Hissar.

Everyone from the church and the Rumeli Hissar household were there to wish the two lovers God's blessing. But young Manoug was the most pleased of all. "I told ya to do it, and ya finally done it," he said triumphantly. "Now kiss her."

"I already have," Aram confided quietly.

"When? I missed it!"

"So did everyone else. But the day I marry her, I will kiss her in public, and you will see it. Look at my face. Do you see the happy glow that love for someone brings? This will happen to you too someday if you'll let it."

Diamondola and Aram's Wedding Photo

Chapter 2

THE WEDDING

Excitement at the Rumeli Hissar household did not subside after the engagement party. Everyone now focused on the wedding date which had been set for September 21. The fact that the day was still 11 months away did not keep anyone from planning and working in their own way for the marriage of their two favorite people. The orphans were happily occupied creating little gifts of love. The girls made hand-embroidered handkerchiefs, doilies, and dish towels, while the boys whittled crude coat hangers and towel racks. Mother Keanides filled her daughter's hope chest with embroidered sheets, pillow cases, table clothes, and dresser scarves. Mrs. Greaves concentrated on the nuptial dinner, planning how she could save a little here and there NOW in order to provide the customary Armenian wedding feast THEN.

Money was very scarce in those days after World War I. There was no income from church members—those once generous saints were either refugees or dead. Money coming from the European Division of Seventh-day Adventists to pay the salaries of the mission workers was both meager and irregular. They were most grateful, however, for what money they received. It was this money that sustained EVERYONE. The mission workers had studied the emergency situation and concluded that the only way they could support the refugees and themselves was to pool their resources. Therefore, the mission workers rented Rumeli Hissar, a huge, rambling old house with a garden, and lived communally with the orphans and refugees. Rumeli Hissar was like a hotel in that it had many rooms and a commercial-size kitchen, dining room, and parlor. The refugees and orphans did the house work and laundry and raised a garden to supplement the food rations. Of course, it was inconvenient for the mission workers to have the long commute to the office each day, but if they did not live sacrificially they could not care for the poor souls who survived the massacre of the Christians. No one complained because of the one-room-per-family set-up or of the food; they were just grateful to be alive and have food and shelter.

Life had been grim for all the members of the Rumeli Hissar household in one way or another during the past six years. The blossoming of love within their group animated their broken spirits and renewed their zest for life. Reveling in the joy of the up-coming wedding would provide 11 months of therapy for them.

The shortage of help at the mission office down town threw the lovers together more than most engaged couples. The first thing in the morning after household worship, they were off to the office with Elder Greaves. Then they had lunch together, did their office work, and went home again in the evening. Sometimes it was difficult for them to concentrate on their work, but being constantly surrounded by a bevy of people helped.

Aram, however, was determined to make their engagement period special for Diamondola. He put a fresh rose on her desk each morning with a little love missive. When they could squeeze in the time, he took her shopping. Since ready-made clothes were nowhere available in Turkey in those days, Aram bought his fiancee choice pieces of material for dresses and coats. Once in awhile they had to stop at the dress maker's for fittings. Aram's eyes sparkled as he viewed Diamondola in the lovely dresses which evolved from the hands of the seamstress.

"You look absolutely stunning in that dainty floral print!" he exclaimed. "Those soft fabrics are far more attractive than the blue serges you usually wear. They emphasize your petite figure most alluringly." Then he sidled up to her and gave her a quick peck on the cheek—when the dressmaker wasn't watching, of course.

"Aram, not here! And I'm not that petite. I'm almost five feet tall and weigh 89 pounds. Besides, you mustn't encourage my vanity," Diamondola laughed, pushing him aside playfully. His compliments made her blush, but she allowed him to continue the practice. It was good to feel loved and admired by a man again. Not just any man—Aram. She felt confident that God wanted them teamed up as His ambassadors. This thought made her happy that she had agreed to marry him.

Outside the fence of Rumeli Hissar, there was no peace and contentment in Turkey. The Turkish economy had not recovered from the financial drain of World War I; so the people were poor. The citizens were restless because no law or order evolved to stabilize the chaotic condition. The people felt that the war had been mismanaged and blamed their old leaders for their lost cause. Civil war loomed on the horizon. Young Mustafa Kemal was emerging as an organized, capable leader. The people rallied to his call, and his "Nationalist Movement" began to gather supporters and momentum. Yet there remained a fear that the rapid changes taking place in Turkey were not all for the best. Modernization was needed, but would religious freedom be a part of the new regime?

Perhaps this was not the best time in history to be getting married. But Diamondola, now 26, and Aram, 36, had never seen good days during their lifetime. At their age, there seemed to be no point in delay. Besides, they were in love. Autumn passed into winter, winter into spring, spring into summer, and it was autumn again. September 21, 1921, the day for the wedding, finally came. The final touches were put on Diamondola's filmy veil and white wedding gown. Aram's new shirt and white bow tie lay pressed and ready on his bed. Chairs were set up in the garden, and flowers decorated a make-shift platform. Elder and Mrs. Erzberger, their special mission friends, had arrived back in

Turkey from their European furlough. Everything and everybody was ready for the event.

Theodora helped her daughter dress for the wedding while Mrs. Erzberger buzzed about putting a stray curl of Diamondola's in place. Elder Erzberger straightened Aram's bow tie. Someone played wedding music on Diamondola's piano, a gift from Ares. Then the couple met in the foyer and walked arm in arm behind the minister and mounted the platform. Little heads bobbed from side to side to get the best view of their beloved couple. The older ladies shed the happy tears one must produce at such an emotional event. Elder Erzberger preached a most impressive sermon and the "I do's" were said. Then, THEN, Aram leaned over and kissed Diamondola. The little girls giggled and the young boys gasped.

Then, during a moment of absolute silence, a loud whisper was heard. "He said he'd do it one day so's I would see it, and he did! He kissed her! People do that when they feel love."

Aram turned, smiled, and winked at Manoug.

Everyone congratulated the bride and groom. But the best congratulation of all for Aram was the spontaneous hug he got from Manoug. At last Manoug's emotional scars seemed to be healing, and he was beginning to feel love. September 21 was not only a beginning of a new life for Diamondola and Aram, but a new beginning for Manoug as well.

Chapter 3

THE FREEDOM FIGHTER

The day after the wedding there was a mission committee meeting which both newly weds were required to attend since Aram was the Union's secretary and Diamondola the treasurer. It was not until two weeks after their wedding that the young couple found time to move Diamondola's things down to Aram's quarters. Probably no one in history had a shorter honeymoon trip, nor as much company while doing it, than did the Ashods. Everyone in the household shared in the task. One person carried a mirror, others the new dresses on hangers, while still others found more feminine gear to adorn the bachelor's quarters. On October 5, Diamondola took up her official residence with Aram. The trek home to mother's was only one flight up, so breaking the home ties was easy.

A week later the Ashods and Erzbergers were invited to a birthday party on the other side of the Golden Horn, a narrow strip of water separating two parts of Constantinople. Parties were rare during those days of austerity, so this was a special treat. The morning of the party Diamondola decided she may as well stay home and translate the mission publication there. Then late in the afternoon, she and Mrs. Erzberger would dress, meet their husbands at the ferry boat landing, and proceed to the party together.

Aram kissed his bride fondly and casually remarked in parting, "Look, Sweetheart, I'd like for you to wear that flowered silk dress at the party tonight. It makes you look like a China doll."

Diamondola stood in the doorway and blew him another kiss as he rounded the corner. His parting words made her feel warm all over. How good it was to be loved and complimented again. For years she had neither time nor desire to think about herself as the attractive, desirable person she really was. She considered pride and vanity two of the seven deadly sins, but she sorted things out and decided that it was not sinful to accept indulgent compliments from Aram.

The chime of the clock interrupted her reverie, reminding her that she should get busy with her translating. After lunch she settled back into her work, accomplishing more than usual. Suddenly she realized that much time had slipped by, and she needed to hurry to be ready to meet Aram and Elder Erzberger at the appointed time. She ran to her closet, pulled out the flowered silk dress, and slipped into it. Then she brushed her brown wavy hair and swept it up into an attractive bun. She looked in the mirror. Maybe she did look like a China doll. Then her eye caught the reflection in the mirror of someone else—Mrs. Erzberger was standing in the doorway watching her.

"Mercy, child!" the good lady exclaimed. "You aren't going to wear that flimsy silk in this October chill, are you?"

"Well, yes, I thought I should," Diamondola answered. "Aram asked me to wear this particular dress. It's one of his favorites," she explained demurely.

"Diamondola, are you going to let Aram boss you around to the extent that he dictates to you what to wear? You've got a good head on your shoulders. You have been independent all these years, making good decisions on your own. Now look at you—married less than three weeks and already you are letting Aram dictate the simplest things, like what you should wear! You are starting out all wrong by catering to his whims. Before you know it, you won't be able to call your soul your own." Mrs. Erzberger delivered herself of this piece of advice free of charge, then turned on her heel and marched on down the hallway. She left Diamondola with a head full of conflicting ideas.

"Now," thought Diamondola, "here is advice from an experienced married lady. She and Elder Erzberger have been happily married for a number of years, and she is not subservient to him. I want to maintain my personhood too, so I'd better assert myself right from the start of our marriage."

Diamondola flew down the hallway and caught up with the sage. "Mrs. Erzberger, what do you suggest I wear?"

"Why something sensible, of course—like a suit or a warm dress."

In a moment Diamondola was back in her room, out of the silk, and into a navy blue serge suit. She never stopped to realize that she had just traded one boss for another.

As the two ladies walked down the road together, Diamondola never felt so independent in her whole life. She had defied Aram's specific "order" and felt quite smug about it. (She had forgotten that it had been only an indulgent request.) She was establishing her own turf. She was determined not to be a submissive house wife like some women in the Middle East.

Down at the ferry landing the women met their husbands. If Aram noticed that Diamondola was not wearing the flowered silk dress, he hardly had time to mention it before his little fireball went into action. She deliberately ignored his warm greeting, mounted the steps, and strode boldly onto the ferry. The attendant waved his arms wildly shouting, "Madame, come back and pay your toll."

Diamondola heard him but ignored him. "Hmph! Just let that big boss Aram take care of that toll for me," she thought as she marched airily on.

"Wait, Darling," Aram called, wasting his breath. "We've got to pay the toll before we can board the ferry."

Diamondola didn't answer. She waited on the far side of the ferry, leaving the embarrassed Aram to pay their tolls and placate the much agitated attendant. Her companions were utterly shocked by Diamondola's irrational behavior. The congenial girl had suddenly undergone a personality reversal. The three rushed after the diminutive despot who stood with her arms folded, leaning against the rail and assuming the defiant air of Richard the Lionhearted. They gazed at her aghast, wondering if Diamondola had taken leave of her senses.

Aram ran up to her. "What is wrong with you, Diamondola?" he asked justifiably disturbed.

"Nothing. Nothing at all," she answered coolly. "But you might as well understand from the start, Aram Ashod, that I am my own person with a good shoulder on my hea..., I mean a good head on my shoulders. And I'll not cater to your every whim."

Mrs. Erzberger overheard the conversation and recoiled as she recognized her speech of the afternoon. How she wished she had kept her mouth shut! But who could have guessed it would turn the sensible Diamondola into a neo-Napoleon?

Aram wisely said nothing to dispute or underscore her statements, though he wondered for all the world what he had said or done to bring this on. He was so stunned that he didn't even dare offer to take her arm as they walked down the street together. He glanced sideways at her, wanting to make sure he had the right woman at his side. He did. No "Laban" had tricked him. But now how could he resolve the mystery which he did not even understand?

During the party, Diamondola moved freely among the guests chatting light-heartedly about nothing. This was so out-of-character for her. She'd always had purpose in her life.

Aram bore patiently with his little bride, while she brushed aside his overtures for reconciliation. The return trip home was as frigid as the weather. Though the cold wind proved that Diamondola was wise to wear a warm suit, she chose to ignore the fact that she could have worn a coat over her silk dress. Just before reaching home, Mrs. Erzberger managed to whisper in

Diamondola's ear, "Don't you think you're carrying this too far?"

Back at Rumeli Hissar the Ashods studied their Sabbath School lesson together. Then Diamondola slithered into bed feeling miserable and guilty. Aram had been very patient with her unreasonable behavior, but she worried that if she apologized to him she would lose the ground she had established. She must guard her independence. She turned her face toward the wall and tried to go to sleep.

Aram wanted to take his bride in his arms and have her tell him what was bothering her. He knew he needed to handle the situation delicately, however, so he simply said, "Good night, Darling. I love you. Ah, are you feeling well?"

Diamondola's arrogance was broken by his kindness. She wanted to ask his forgiveness, but how could she explain her actions? The whole thing now seemed so absurd. In her misery, she answered contritely, "I'm well."

Aram sensed a mellowing in her attitude, but he did not dare disturb the peace to comment.

Diamondola missed the warmth of his arms about her and their goodnight kiss. She wished she could think of a face-saving solution. She thought, "I've never been more wicked, and Aram has never been more righteous."

Sleep finally overcame Diamondola and gave her a respite from her guilty conscience. Suddenly a voice spoke to her saying, "Colossians 3:18." She arose with a start. It wasn't Aram's voice. She stared into the darkness trying to recall what that verse said. When she heard the voice again, she knew she couldn't go back to sleep until she found out what Colossians 3:18 said. The matches, lamp, and Bible were on the dresser beside Aram. She hated to disturb him, but her anxiety left her no choice.

She touched him. "Aram Dear, what does Colossians 3:18 say?"

17

Aram stirred himself from his restless sleep. "I, ah, don't remember."

"Aram," she said gently, "a voice gave me this verse. I really need to know what it says. Would you please light the lamp and read it to me?"

"Of course, Sweetie." Aram could not refuse the pleading little voice of his beloved. He got up, lit the lamp, opened the Bible and read, "Wives submit yourselves to your own husbands, as it is fit in the Lord." Aram closed the Bible, blew out the lamp, crawled back into bed, and made no comment.

Diamondola felt condemned. She remembered now what the next verse said, "Husbands, love your wives and be not bitter against them." Aram had certainly followed the Biblical injunction. He was not bitter against her, although he certainly had cause to be. He had continued to demonstrate his love to her even when she rebuffed him.

Diamondola sat on the edge of the bed and laid a hand on his cheek. "Dearest," she began tearfully, "I'm sorry for the way I've treated you tonight. I know you aren't that way—you know, the kind of man who would lord it over me. You have always treated me as an equal, and I love and respect you too. I will follow Paul's advice. Please forgive me."

In a moment Aram had his bride in his arms. "Of course, I forgive you. But could you give me a clue as to what brought on this—ah, this attitude?"

Then she told him about the dress and Mrs. Erzberger's advice. They laughed together about Diamondola's over-reaction.

"Oh, this is so funny," Aram said as he wiped tears from his eyes. "You surely had me confused; I had no clue as to what was bothering you. But I don't foresee any problem here. I agree that we should each keep our individuality; yet there will probably be times when each of us will need to make some concessions. I believe these adjustments will come easily and naturally for us.

We have made Jesus the center of our home, and we are both dedicated to being God's ambassadors to the Middle East. Let's make our home an example of Christian unity and a little bit of heaven on earth. And," he added jokingly, repeating Diamondola's words, "as an ardent admirer of that 'good head on your shoulders,' I never expected you to 'cater to my every whim.' I think that head is very pretty—even to those saucy little lips."

Then he kissed her tenderly.

Chapter 4

THEIRS NOT TO QUESTION WHY

The Larsons arrived in Constantinople during the late fall of 1921 with the money to establish an orphanage in the city. This project had been voted during the 1920 Seventh-day Adventist European Conference. Diamondola had written a series of 13 stories depicting the plight of the Adventist refugees and war orphans. These stories were then read throughout North America. The American Adventists responded generously to the "Near East Relief Fund." Now, a year and a half later, the money was in hand to initiate the project.

The Ashods and Larsons, both newly wed couples, became close friends immediately. Together they worked for permits to establish the orphanage; they rented a building and prepared it for occupancy. As the winter of 1922 progressed, they realized the facility would be needed sooner than anticipated.

Following World War I, the Allies stationed Greek occupational forces throughout sections of Turkey. Therefore, the Christians, who had survived the atrocities inflicted upon them during the war, thought it was now safe to return to their homes in the interior and reclaim their property. They did not foresee that a new wave of terror was about to descend upon them.

Turkey was ripe for a revolution. The disgruntled citizens had given their all for the war effort and had lost everything. They blamed their leaders. In May 1919, young Mustafa Kemal (Ataturk), hero of the Dardenelles, swept into Samsun, a port on the Black Sea in northern Turkey. The people rallied behind him and his guerilla forces. Kemal's slogan, "Turkey for the Turks", incited their national pride and inspired their loyalty to him. Kemal's revolutionary movement rapidly gained momentum throughout Turkey.

The Turks hated the Greek occupational forces and anyone who supported them. Since the old central government had plundered and killed the Christians for over a quarter of a century, the Turkish revolutionaries assumed that the Christians would take revenge and fight with the Greek occupational forces against them. Therefore, Kemal and his band swept suddenly and relentlessly upon one city after another, driving out the Greek forces. The Greco-Turkish citizens fled on the heels of the retreating occupational troops. Kemal's Nationalist forces then plundered the deserted homes and barracks, capturing materials and ammunition to bolster their fight. The central government was too weak and too weary to stop them. The pillage and plunder engulfed the countryside as one village after another fell into the hands of the Nationalist forces. Hundreds of Christians were killed in the wake.

Early in 1922 word of the new wave of atrocities reached the Christians in Constantinople via the few fortunate ones who escaped. The Adventists prayed for the safety of their fellow believers and the three ministers whom they knew would be special targets. Nine Adventist ministers had already been killed. Everyone was especially concerned for the safety of Diran Tcharakian at Iconium. He was a powerful preacher and success-ful soul winner. The members had doubted the wisdom of Elder Frauchiger and the mission board in sending this indomitable apostle to the interior of Turkey when the whole country was seething in turmoil. It seemed like a needless risk to place this valuable leader in such a vulnerable situation as he would encounter in Iconium. He, a refined, university ex-professor, would draw the attention of authorities. But when Elder Frauchiger asked Tcharakian to "go to Iconium to firm up the work," he never questioned his mission. Like Paul, taking his fateful trip to Jerusalem, Tcharakian bid his friends a tearful farewell and left. Perhaps he had a premonition that he would never see them again.

Tcharakian left after the war in 1918. Word filtered back to the mission of his marvelous evangelistic successes. Next, they heard that he was arrested, beaten, stripped of his clothing, imprisoned, tormented, and starved. He bore his abuse as a patient, faithful witness. Many of his letters reached their destination because his jailers, who liked Tcharakian, mailed them for him. Those Paulian letters brought courage to the believers and remained treasured epistles in their hands. When Tcharakian began converting his fellow prisoners, the jailers released him. They felt his influence there was too dangerous, and they liked him too well to kill him. Tcharakian should probably have fled for Constantinople then, but nothing daunted his priceless faith and courage, so he returned to his ministry.

When Diamondola and Aram got married, they had hoped Tcharakian would respond to their wedding invitation. The three had been special friends for many years. In God's providence, their paths seemed to cross at appointed times. First, Aram persuaded Professor Tcharakian to leave atheism and believe in the living God. (Aram was not a Seventh-day Adventist at this time.) Diamondola translated the sermons that brought the Third Angel's Message of Revelation to Tcharakian, which led him to join the Adventist church. Next, Tcharakian brought the full truth to Aram which resulted in his conversion to Adventism. Diamondola encouraged Professor Tcharakian to resign his teaching position at the National University to become an Adventist minister at 1/20th of his salary. When Diamondola died of typhus in 1919, it was Tcharakian who had the faith to ask God to resurrect her, even though she had been dead for six hours. After Tcharakian's wife and family left him, Diamondola and Aram became his family. Information about their friend Diran Tcharakian reached the Ashods in April, 1922. Refugees arriving at the just-barely-opened orphanage confirmed a report that Tcharakian, along with other Christians, had been captured in Iconium and marched off to the Syrian Desert to perish.*

The refugees who managed to escape flocked to the Adventist orphanage in Constantinople. As the Ashods and Larsons watched the building swell to overflowing with the hapless victims, they marveled that God had put it into the hearts of the church leaders to prepare this center of refuge at the exact time it was needed. It was a miracle! The funds had been collected in 1921, the building had been prepared during the winter of 1922, and the refugees arrived in April of 1922. The orphans, the aged, and the dying wrecks of humanity flooded the facility beyond its capacity, but no one was turned away. During the General Conference Session of 1922, additional funds were sent to Turkey to assist with the refugee emergency program. Some exiles used the refuge only as a way-station until they could arrange visas to immigrate to other countries; for others, it became a permanent home because they had no money or relatives to help them move on.

Among the refugees arriving at the orphanage was Diamondola's Uncle Sava. He was a God-send. They desperately needed a maintenance man, and Sava could do it all—plumbing, carpentry, masonry, and any other fix-it job. He kept the orphanage functioning smoothly. But what Sava probably enjoyed the most was being Grandpa to the children and an ear for the older folks.

Diamondola's childhood playmate, Zabelle from Brousa, found her way to the orphanage. She had become a Seventh-day Adventist. Since Zabelle was a very cheerful, motherly Christian, they made her the matron for the school. How the children loved her!

While the orphanage became a little haven for the Christians who reached Constantinople, the news about Christians in other parts of the country was alarming. The British and French forces withdrew from Turkey, leaving Christians stranded in the Nationalist's territory. In their haste to leave, the foreign forces left ammunition which fell into the hands of the Nationalists. This ammunition was used to kill the Christians and some of the occupational troops. The Kemalist movement, which was now in its third and most expansive year, was sweeping the remaining opposition into the sea. Christians fled to seaport towns where some of them persuaded or bribed sea captains of ships to smuggle them aboard. Others fled south to Lebanon.

Smyrna (now Izmir), one of the largest seaport towns, was flooded with refugees. There the Kemalist army closed in on them, forcing them to the beaches. They huddled together in groups—hungry, thirsty, sick, frightened, and cold—dreading the hour when they would be slaughtered.

On the night that the genocide began, the British navy was anchored inside the harbor. Hundreds of desperate, strong young men risked the terrors of the deep and swam through the waves to the sides of the ships. Exhausted and floating on their backs, the young men begged to be taken aboard. But their pitiful pleas went unheeded by the British sailors who had been instructed by their officers to pick up NO ONE. The ships' captains had wired London regarding the situation. The orders came back that they were not to interfere in Turkey's internal affairs. Rescuing these Christian youth, they reasoned, might be considered interference. Thousands of Christian youth perished that night by the sides of the ships of a Christian nation. In the morning, the waves lapped their bloated bodies to the shore. Could the ships' captains ever erase from their memories the night they gave the orders not to lower ropes to save the young men?

News of the atrocious death of another of Diamondola's friends made her sick with pity. The Orthodox Patriarch, with whom she and Elder Frauchiger had studied the book of Revelation, had been transferred from the capitol to Izmir. The Bishop advised him to flee Izmir on any ship that would take him, but he refused to leave his flock who could not get the same privilege. When the Nationalists entered the city, they seized the Greek Patriarch, killed him, tied his body to a carriage and drug it through the streets for the edification of the Christian refugees. His heroism is commemorated by a statue in a museum in Athens.

Amid the excitement of the new orphanage, the carnage of the Christians, and the intense political upheaval, Aram, Mr.Larson, and Elder Erzberger were called to Bulgaria for a Union Committee meeting. The Ashods never questioned the wisdom of this trip. In days such as these, the prudent (or faithless) may have worried that the men would never return from the convention, or that the executions might reach Constantinople in their absence. But through the years of trial and deliverance that they had already survived, Diamondola and Aram had learned not to question why. The call of the mission was a call from God. Aram left his bride of less than a year and went with the other men to the European meetings—just another assignment for God's ambassador.

*The story of Tcharakian's demise was told to the author in 1962 by Dr. Garo, one of the men from Iconium who was exiled with him. Garo was one of the few who escaped from the soldiers. He fled to Beirut, became a dentist, and joined the Adventist church. His story about Tcharakian is as follows:

On June 21, 1921 the Kemalist forces suddenly surrounded Iconium. No Christian had time to escape or send messages to friends in other places. Elder Tcharakian was captured along with other Christians who were grouped into units of ten, and marched into exile. As he plodded along the rugged, unchartered trails on the death march into the Syrian Desert, he ever bore a witness of love and comfort to his wretched companions. He preached the love of Jesus to his captors who drove the starved and weary sufferers at bayonet point across the snow-clad mountains and blistering deserts and plains. They were nearing the Tigris River when Tcharakian, burning with fever, was unable to drag himself further. He was much loved by the exiles. They carried him or placed him across the back of a horse, hoping he would survive. But one night as they camped on the bank of a river, they knew that Tcharakian wouldn't live. In the morning his companions laid him gently in a meadow, believing he was dead. With a last burst of energy, he opened his eyes, exhorted them to love one another, have faith in God, and forgive their persecutors. He then breathed his last and was buried in a shallow grave on Friday afternoon, July 8, 1921.

Many of the exiles were inspired and impressed by the saintly preacher. A non-Adventist paper had this to say of him: "During the whole journey, Diran Tcharakian was inspired by the words of God. He was against any fanatical feeling and any spirit of revenge...he showed forgiveness to his persecutors. His faith was never shaken, and he never let the Bible leave his hands."

When the news of Tcharakian's death reached the Adventist community, they mourned the passing of God's four-star general. Though the temptation to doubt God's wisdom was sometimes great, they knew theirs was not to question why. The memory of Diran Tcharakian inspired them to pray for a portion of his faith and power. Sometimes they wondered if they had depended too much upon his matchless faith and failed to tap the resources of omnipotent power and wisdom for themselves.

Chapter 5

TO GO OR TO STAY?

The establishment of new national boundaries in the Middle East following World War I necessitated the reorganization of the mission work in those countries as well. The delegates returned from the Bulgarian Adventist Council with the disturbing news that the Levant Union Mission, which comprised the countries of the East Mediterranean area with headquarters in Istanbul, had been dissolved. Now the leaders of the Adventist mission work in each country would report directly to the European Division: Otto Schubert for Bulgaria; Nils Zerner for Syria and Lebanon; George Keough for Egypt; and Greaves for Greece. Turkey would never again be the center of the Adventist mission work in the Middle East.

The tyranny of the great Ottoman Empire, once the pride of the Turks and their Sultans, was toppled by the Allies during WW I. The peace treaty forced upon them gave the mandate of Lebanon and Syria to the French, while Palestine, Iraq, Jordan, and Egypt were placed under British control. The humiliation of losing control over the eastern Mediterranean countries seared the egos of the Turks, but the greatest affront was having the occupational forces of their life-long enemies, the Greeks, set up throughout their country. This indignity did not last long. By 1923, Mustafa Kemal and his Nationalist troops had ousted the Greek forces and claimed "Turkey for the Turks". If they couldn't have an empire, they would, at least, have their own country for themselves. Capable and popular, Mustafa became the

27

undisputed leader of the new republic and became known throughout the world as Kemal Ataturk, the father of the Turks.

The Nationalists soon discovered that rebuilding the nation from an oligarchy to a republic was a horrendous task. The mostly uneducated citizens, steeped in tradition and the old ways, were unprepared for Ataturk's sweeping, 20th century, modernization reforms: 1) He decreed that no new Moslem mosques or Christian churches could be built. 2) He Latinized the alphabet which revolutionized the whole literary program for the schools, libraries, and those who read the Arabic script. 3) He had the veils removed from the women which the Moslems felt interfered with their religion. 4) He adopted the Nansen Plan for population exchange which threatened the non-Turkish citizens with expatriation. (Nansen was a Norwegian diplomat who arranged for hundreds of prisoners of war to be returned to their own country following WW I. Furthermore, he proposed that it would be better for people of a certain nationality to live in their own country; that is, Greeks should move to Greece, Turks should move to Turkey, etc.) 5) Ataturk changed the name of the capital, Constantinople, a Greek word, to Istanbul, a Turkish word. To the populace, it seemed that Ataturk instituted new reforms almost daily, keeping them in a constant state of suspense.

Expatriation, the core issue in the Nansen Plan, threatened the security of Diamondola and her mother more than any of the other reforms. The Greeks born in Turkey since the Balkan Wars of 1912–13 would have to go to Greece, and Turks born in Greece after 1913 would have to transfer to Turkey. On the surface this appeared like a wise solution. It should end the constant bickering between Turkey and Greece. However, for the hundreds of people involved, expatriation caused many complications. Parents with young children born after 1913 would be forced to leave their businesses, land, and homes behind to take their children out of the country. Furthermore, people who could not produce proper legal documents indicating citizenship before 1912 would have to leave Turkey, even though they were born in

Turkey and had lived there all their lives. Few people had birth certificates in those days because it was not considered important to register the event with the government. Therefore, unless the Greek was a property owner or had a birth certificate, he would find it was almost impossible to produce satisfactory papers. Diamondola and her mother fell into this category. Neither of them had birth certificates or owned property. Aram, being an Armenian with a birth certificate, was exempt from this law, so he could stay in Turkey legally.

"Well, I guess I'll be going to Greece," Diamondola told Aram one day as she entered his office. "I suppose it would be nice to live in a Christian country with my sisters Alexandra and Susanna. God knows it hasn't been easy being a Christian worker in Moslem Turkey. In the 1890's, more than 100,000 Armenians were martyred. The Cilician massacre of 1909 saw another 30,000 killed. God only knows how many millions have died since 1915. (Taken from *Martyrdom and Rebirth*, pp. 20, 21.) Who knows what new edict issued in Turkey will affect us?"

"I don't know, Darling," Aram replied, pushing himself away from his desk. "But killing off political or religious enemies has been a historical trend ever since Adam sold out to Lucifer. The Egyptians did it. So did the Israelites, Assyrians, Babylonians, Persians, Greeks, and Romans. Even Christians persecuted other Christians during the Dark Ages."

"Are you going soft on the Turks now?" Diamondola questioned suspiciously.

"Well, not really. I'm just saying that the Turks aren't the only ones who have committed atrocities. I'll concede that it would be nice to get out of Turkey—things are not stable here yet. Any day a new law could be enacted that would exterminate Christians in Constan..., I mean, Istanbul."

"So," Diamondola contended, "why don't we leave now? If statistics count for anything, we're not accomplishing much here."

"Yes we are," Aram countered. "We've helped hundreds of people..."

"But the reports show no increase in church membership," argued Diamondola.

"Are you more concerned about statistics than souls, Diamondola? That's not like you. We've baptized many new converts. It's just that they emigrate almost immediately to other countries, so an increase doesn't show up on the books." Aram sobered, put his elbows on the table, and held his head between his hands. "I'll admit some of this is getting to me too. Every time I purchase tickets and say farewell to our people seeking asylum in other lands, I get an empty feeling. Oh, I'm happy for them. They're leaving behind a painful past and facing a better future. But when I watch their ships pull away from the docks, I feel abandoned. It's like I'm seeing the last life boat pull away from a sinking ship, and I'm left standing on the bridge."

"Oh, Aram," Diamondola said as she slid herself onto his lap and laid her head against his cheek. "I didn't know you were suffering pangs of separation too. But it's no wonder. Its discouraging being the only Adventist ministers in Turkey—no one here with whom we can share our burdens. First, the Erzbergers and Greaves left us in 1922. Then in April 1923, just one year after the orphanage was established, it was moved to Greece. With it went our good friends, the Larsons, Uncle Sava, Zabelle, your favorite orphan Manoug, and the other children. Even my mother went with them."

"But she'll be back. She just went to visit your sisters," Aram added trying to console his wife. Then Aram smiled, "I have some good news for you."

"What? Tell me quick!" Diamondola begged, looking into his eyes.

"Look at this telegram we just received. It says that the Grins from Switzerland will soon arrive to work with us. We won't be alone anymore. And, with apologies, it also says that I'm to take over the books for the Turkish mission, relieving the capable Mrs. Diamon..."

"Oh, good!" Diamondola exclaimed, leaping from his lap and dancing about the room. "I'm glad the Grins are coming, and happier still that I'll get rid of that bookkeeping. You're the one who is trained in accounting and will do the best job. Now I can just relax at home and be an ordinary housewife."

"Not so fast, my Dear. Hear the rest of the telegram. You are to continue your translating and secretarial work, and I'll do some translating too. We'll have to promote the literature work since that's the only ministry left in Turkey."

Diamondola sobered, remembering the time from 1908 to 1914 when the new constitution proclaimed "liberty, justice, equality, fraternity." During those golden years the work advanced rapidly. Ministers and colporteurs evangelized villages, the office shelves were stocked with literature in many languages which was then packaged and sent out to the field. Now the colporteurs, ministers, and most of the members had either died or emigrated. The literature shelves were empty, the churches were in ruins, and the Christian schools and homes had been confiscated. The future looked grim. Even though the Grins were coming to Turkey, Diamondola had no assurance that she would be able to stay and work with them. She was still without papers verifing her Turkish citizenship. They had prayed that if they should stay, God would solve this problem for them.

Days turned into weeks. As expatriation time drew nearer, Diamondola's hopes of remaining in Turkey faded. The possibility of leaving had become a reality for her, and she had adjusted to the idea. She thought she might as well start eliminating her non-essential possessions since they would soon be moving.

One rainy day she began sifting through a mass of mementos she had stuffed into her old trunk. Down near the bottom she found a yellowed envelope that had not been disturbed in 10 years. On the outside she had written "Balkan War certificates and decorations." She opened it and fingered through the assortment of papers. There was the street car pass that the government had given to hospital volunteers and the arm band she had worn as a practical nurse in the army. Here was the Turkish Red Crescent certificate, which was the Ottoman Empire's equivalent of the western world's Red Cross. Beneath it lay the certificate from the Ministry of War, expressing the government's appreciation for her nursing services during the Balkan Wars. Abruptly she paused and focused her eyes upon the date, "Summer of 1913". Suddenly the importance of this paper dawned upon her. Here was positive proof that she had not only lived in Turkey before 1913 but had voluntarily served the government.

Diamondola jumped to her feet, scattering papers and keepsakes in all directions. She dynamited down the steps, fired with excitement. "I've got it, I've got it," she yelled racing through the house to find Aram.

Aram grabbed her arm as she flew by him. "WHAT have you got? Now stop your leaping about, calm down, and tell me what you've got."

"I've got the answer to our prayers right here in my hand. This certificate anti-dates the 1913 deadline set for expatriation," she said as her shaky finger pointed out several spots on the paper. "See, this proves that I served as a volunteer during the Balkan Wars. That should entitle me to Turkish citizenship. We prayed that God would show us whether to go or to stay. This paper says we STAY."

A thrill ran through Aram's body, giving him goose bumps. He studied the document. "It's God's answer," he murmured reverently.

The next morning Diamondola and Aram presented the certificate along with her request to remain in Turkey as a natural-born citizen. Her request was granted, and they stayed in Turkey.

Was it a coincident that she, a secretary/translator/bookkeeper, had been asked to serve as a nurse aid in the Balkan Wars? Was it a coincidence that she had saved the certificate and then found it just when it was needed? No. It was part of God's plan. With Him there are no accidents. His timing is perfect and His plans impeccable.

Chapter 6

STAYING BY THE STUFF

"About 400 men went up with David, while 200 stayed with the stuff." 1 Samuel 25:13.

Diamondola and Aram "stayed by the stuff" and held the church work together after their associates left. At times they felt swamped with the mission and local church work, the accounts, translating, publishing, correspondence, and a myriad of other details. They gladly welcomed the new Turkish mission president, M. C. Grin, and his family during the summer of 1924. Grin launched right into his duties. This freed the Ashods to give more Bible studies which was the main reason they had remained in Turkey in the first place.

One evening Diamondola answered a knock on her door. She was stunned when she saw it was Elizabeth, a nurse with whom she had worked as a volunteer in the military hospital in 1913.

The ladies flew into each other's arms, tears of joy streamed down their faces. "Where have you been these past eight years?" Diamondola finally managed to ask. "I hadn't heard from you, so I thought you were dead."

"I was all but dead a number of times. It's a long story—too painful to rehearse the details. When I left my things with you in 1916, I planned to make only a brief visit to my home in Iconium. I hadn't even settled in when the deportation decree was effected. My family, what was left of it from the other massacres, was split up again. I'm sure none of them survived this one. On the death

34

march, I was starved, beaten, abused, and..." Elizabeth's voice trailed off as she choked back sobs. She regained her composure and continued. "I was left for dead. Then a kind Moslem family found me. I lived with them for several years, and I loved them. But since I didn't want to remain in a harem, I escaped and found my way here. Don't ask me more." Tears clouded Elizabeth's eyes.

Diamondola led her into their apartment. "Come into my bedroom. I want to show you something," Diamondola said as she flipped open the lid of a trunk.

"Oh! Oh my! I can't believe it," Elizabeth squealed. "It's my bedding and, and my clothes. Oh Diamondola, I never thought I'd ever see them again."

"I aired and moth-balled them twice a year," Diamondola told her. "I didn't give up on the possibility of your coming back."

"After what I've been through, I can hardly believe such wonderful people still exist. What kind of person are you to be faithful to a trust for so many years?" Elizabeth asked as she sorted through her belongings.

"A Christian, I hope," Diamondola answered simply.

"I want what you've got. Will you teach me about Jesus?" Elizabeth asked.

Elizabeth stayed with the Ashods until she found work at the hospital. Every night they studied the Bible together. In a few months Elizabeth accepted Jesus as her best Friend. She was baptized secretly one moonlit night in the Marmara Sea. When she accumulated sufficient funds she emigrated to the United States. Ashods were sorry to see another friend leave them, but they were thankful their lives had touched long enough to help Elizabeth re-establish her faith in humanity and God.

Next, God led the Ashods to Marie Amirou*, a woman of questionable morals. She ran a boarding house for men, but like Mary Magdalene, she was searching, longing for a better life. When the Ashods offered to teach her the Bible, she grasped the opportunity. She was thrilled to learn how much God loved even women like her. She changed her life completely, was baptized in the Marmara Sea, left her old work, and became a governess for a wealthy Turkish family. Marie was fluent in French, Turkish, and Greek. She had a good education, but being a Greek, a woman, and a Christian limited her job opportunities. Marie was filled with missionary zeal. She always carried a supply of literature to give away. Every Sabbath in church she gave an encouraging testimony or experience she had had during the week.

"She's another reason God arranged for us to 'stay by the stuff'," Diamondola confided to Aram.

Then there was Victoria, a childhood playmate of Diamondola's from Brousa. After many years of separation, the two ran across each other in downtown Istanbul (the new Turkish name for Constantinople). After the tell-me-what's-happened-to-you conversation lulled, Diamondola tried to interest Victoria in Bible studies, but Victoria was too occupied with her personal problems.

"Diamondola," she complained, "my husband, Hagop Yaridjian, is not caring for me and our four children as he should. I don't know what I would do if it were not for the attention and support Artin gives me. It is Artin who loves and cares for us, pays our bills, and..."

"And who is Artin?" Diamondola asked.

"He is a relative of Hagop's. He's such a wonderful man." And Victoria went on, elaborating on Artin's fine qualities and discrediting Hagop.

A few days later, Artin, having learned of Victoria's contact with Diamondola, came secretly to Ashods' house. After the introductions and some meaningless chit-chat, he got to the core of his mission. "Look," he began, "I have been supporting Victoria and her children financially because she always begs for help. But I have a future of my own to consider, so I don't want to have anything more to do with them. Will you please try to reconcile Hagop and Victoria?"

Diamondola sucked in her breath, suspecting that Victoria's problem had several tentacles; however, she agreed to try. Artin was satisfied and slipped away in the darkness.

As soon as possible, the Ashods met with Hagop and Victoria.

"She accuses me of neglect in order to justify her infidelity," Hagop complained. "What's more, she's in love with Artin."

"Are you?" Aram prodded. "This will break up your home and family."

After several hours of emotional discussion, Victoria admitted that she was in love with Artin but promised to reform. Ashods prayed with the couple and left around midnight.

Hagop was thankful for the Ashods' Christian interest and began Bible studies. Soon he and the three oldest children were attending church. Victoria, however, always managed some excuse to stay home and avoided any spiritual instruction that might prick her conscience.

A few weeks later, Artin paid a second visit to Ashods. "Victoria is very ill and in the hospital," he informed them. "I can't afford to help her."

Again the Ashods rallied to his plea. They collected what money they could from neighbors and church members and then filled in the deficit themselves to finish paying for Victoria's hospital bills. Hagop was most thankful for the concerned Christians who helped him through this crisis. Victoria, however, remained unimpressed, aloof, and depressed.

On Artin's third visit, he begged the Ashods to get Victoria off his back and reconcile her with Hagop. He assured them that he had no affection for Victoria, although he was aware of her infatuation for him. He wanted the Ashods to inform Victoria that there was no more money or visits forthcoming from him.

This time the Ashods visited Victoria when she was alone at her home. They relayed Artin's message as gently and tactfully as possible. Victoria flew into a screaming, crying rage, insisting that Artin still loved her. After several nerve-racking hours the

Ashods finally got Victoria calmed down, and she seemed convinced that Artin really wanted to break off their relationship. She agreed to forget Artin and concentrate on Hagop and the children.

Then Victoria excused herself and went to the kitchen on the pretext of getting some refreshments for the Ashods. At that point, Diamondola and Aram began to relax, supposing that their stressful mission had been accomplished. But they hardly had time to offer a silent prayer of thanks to God for His help in this delicate matter before they were rocked to their feet with an ear-splitting shriek and commotion in the backyard. Ashods flew through the house, bruising themselves as they squeezed through the back door together, and landed in the yard where the action was.

"Victoria has jumped into the well," shouted the distraught neighbor.

"Oh, God, what next?" groaned Aram, begging for heavenly assistance.

The neighbor man leaped over the fence with a rope. "Here, I'll tie this securely around me, and you'll have to pull us up when I get her," he told Aram as he lowered himself into the well.

Aram, still in shock, nodded. With adrenalin pumping Atlas-like power through his body, Aram was able to lift both the man and the unconscious Victoria to the top of the well. An ambulance soon arrived and took the suicide victim to the hospital.

Before the Ashods could recover from this turn of events, the police arrived to question them and make a report.

"Oh, will the complications of this day never end?" Diamondola moaned. "I was only trying to salvage the marriage of my childhood friend and interest her in spiritual things."

"Me too. Ah, Diamondola, did, did we pray about this?" Aram worried.

"Of course, but we weren't given any clue as to the results."

When bedtime came, the Ashods had insomnia. The whole afternoon had been so unsettling, and the scene of the wet, limp Victoria kept flashing before them.

Restful sleep had still not enveloped them when the police banged loudly on their door, informing them that they must appear in court the next day.

"I declare! I do believe there is a conspiracy here to age us before our time," muttered Aram. "After our stressful counseling session with Victoria, I wasn't at all prepared for her grand finale. Then the police interrogation kept my blood pressure at an all-time high. And now, lest my racing heart simmer down to super fast, the police call again to stir it up."

"I think we need to share our heart condition, Aram. While yours is racing, mine has almost stopped." Diamondola sat on the edge of the bed dazed, clutching her arms, and rocking back and forth. "I never imagined that so many calamitous events could be packed into 10 hours. Now we can spend the rest of the night worrying about the accusations that might be brought against us tomorrow. You know how people can twist things. We could be sent to jail for, ah, for who knows what. I'm not enthusiastic about that prospect."

Aram stopped pacing the floor. "Look here, Darling, we're in partnership with God, aren't we? By a miracle He arranged for us to stay here in Turkey, didn't He? He'll teach us what we should say in court tomorrow, won't He?"

Aram's positive thinking was good, but it did not completely alleviate their apprehension.

The next day things went well in court. Then they visited Victoria at the hospital, and things did not go well. She insisted that no one could destroy the ardent love she and Artin shared and demanded that the Ashods stay out of her affairs.

A few days later, Victoria left the hospital. She went home, packed her things, took the youngest child, and moved to Artin's place. She stunned everyone further by revealing that her youngest child was Artin's. Victoria was full of surprises.

There was more for the Ashods to do now. They helped Hagop and the three oldest children adjust to living without the wife and mother they loved. Diamondola taught the 12 year-old girl how to keep house and cook.

But Victoria wasn't finished using the Ashods. This time she chose not to face them directly. She sent her aunt to beg Diamondola to persuade Hagop to give Victoria a divorce. Diamondola felt she could not conscientiously do this. She knew Hagop was sending pleading messages to Victoria, entreating her to return home. He loved her and her youngest child. He was willing to forgive and forget, but Victoria remained adamant. She wanted only Artin and his child, not Hagop and their children.

One day Diamondola went to Hagop's house to help his daughter with some laundry and mending. Quite unexpectedly Victoria's aunt appeared. She was obviously in a cantankerous mood and spoiling for a fight. She immediately began to rail at Diamondola for not convincing Hagop to give Victoria a divorce. Diamondola remained Christian calm and explained her stand on the matter. Now the aunt's temper waxed hotter and hotter. Presently, the demon in her broke loose, and the enraged, gorilla-like woman pounced on little Diamondola, pummeling and kneading her with clenched fists.

"Dear God," Diamondola prayed, "she's going to make pulp of me unless You help me, QUICK!" In a moment, she wrested herself from her blubbery foe and sped from the scene of battle. "A few more experiences like that could discourage me from helping Victoria anymore," she confided to Aram as she treated her bruises.

Diamondola would gladly have endured the mauling and abuse if she could only help Victoria find peace and salvation. But there was no place for God in Victoria's life. She lived only to fulfill her personal lust and selfish desires. The Ashods were reluctant to give up on her, but for the present they acknowledged defeat.

"Well, if it's any consolation for us," Aram sighed, "Jesus himself wasn't 100% successful. The four out of six we wrested from Satan's grasp is quite satisfying. Hagop and the three children are certainly faithful Christians and are so appreciative of anything we do."

"For them," Diamondola commented, "I'm glad we stayed in Turkey."

The Usuljuoglu family presented the Ashods with a different kind of challenge. Mrs. Usuljuoglu and her mother attended the cottage meetings Ashods held in their area. When the ladies decided to keep the Sabbath, Mr. Usuljuoglu, a member of another Protestant church, was furious. He opposed and perse-cuted his wife in many ways. He threatened to break every window in the Adventist church, which was rather ironic. The Adventists had never owned a church in Istanbul. They were currently meeting in the dark basement of the Armenian Protestant Church. Since there were almost no windows in the basement, damage would have been minimal.

Mrs. Usuljuoglu never gave up her faith or her effort to reason with her husband. At last in anger, he agreed, "All right. You bring your Seventh-day Adventist preacher here, and I'll bring my Protestant preacher. We'll see who has the truth."

"But truth isn't up for debate. The Word of God is truth, and we can't argue with that," his wife reasoned.

But Mr. Usuljuoglu insisted upon the confrontation and arranged to have his minister meet Aram at their house on a certain date. Aram kept the appointment but the Protestant minis-ter did not. This distressed Mr. Usuljuoglu but he determined to try again. The next time two Protestant ministers and a member of their church board showed up to face Aram. When the church board member saw his ministers losing the debate, he started ridiculing and insulting the Adventists in a most debasing manner. This behavior angered Mr. Usuljuoglu. He threw the

41

Bible to the floor exclaiming, "What kind of book is this? You read the same verses and reach different conclusions. There is only one right way! What is TRUTH?"

That experience shook the confidence of Mr. Usuljuoglu in his church. When his ministers could not support their beliefs with scripture, they had lowered themselves to insults. This act proved to Mr. Usuljuoglu that they could not support their doctrines from the Bible. He allowed his wife and mother-in-law to be baptized and started to study the Bible with the Ashods. Shortly he too was baptized. Later the two sons and daughter joined the church, making them a united family again. Then they emigrated to Greece where the family was a big asset to the church.

Bodos and Andreas were pickle makers by trade, but they sold alcoholic beverages on the side to supplement their income. Both attended the Ashods' cottage meetings, but Andreas soon rejected the message. He did not want to give up his alcohol, nor the sales of it. Bodos, on the other hand, was thrilled with the message, accepted it, and obeyed it. When the temperance issue was presented he went home and dumped his barrels of wine onto the street. The smell of the bubbly beverage permeated the neighborhood. People flocked into the street and cursed Bodos for "this foolish waste." But Bodos felt good inside. He knew he had done the right thing, and all their ridicule fell on deaf ears. A few weeks later he was baptized and proved to be a very faithful member.

One day in church Diamondola read her treasurer's report giving, among other things, the figure for the birthday thank offerings. The idea of giving a thank offering for another year of life never occurred to Bodos, but he liked the plan. Sunday morning he arrived at the office where Aram was catching up on the bookkeeping. Under his arm Bodos carried a large bundle. "Here, Brother Ashod," he said pushing the bundle at Aram. "My birthday is already past, but I want to give a thank offering anyway. I have no money, so please take this."

Aram eyed the sack suspiciously as Bodos peeled back the folds. Then a huge brown rooster emerged and strutted across the desk. During the next half hour, the rooster had a great time causing havoc in the office while alluding the men.

They finally captured him, stuffed him back into the sack, and took him to the market where he brought a good price. Bodos was pleased with his offering.

Mrs. Nalkranian also studied with the Ashods. When she decided to be baptized her husband had no objection until her "infernal Sabbath-keeping" interfered with her helping him in his business operations. At last the contention grew so strong that he told her either she must give up the Sabbath or leave home. She instructed the children how to manage the house and help their father. Then she packed her bags. Emotion erupted everywhere in the home. The children wept inconsolably and begged their father to allow their mother to stay and keep the Sabbath, but he was adamant. The leave-taking became a heart-rending scene as Mrs. Nalkranian walked down the road carrying her two suitcases. At the corner, she stopped and looked back. Her body was shaking with grief as she blew them a final kiss. Mr. Nalkranian could stand it no longer. He ran after his wife, drew her into his arms, and wept.

"Dear One," he said, holding her close, "don't go. I never realized that God could mean so much to anyone. You were actually willing to give up everything—me, your security, your home, and your children in order to obey Him. You have some special relationship with God. I wish I had your faith."

Mr. Nalkranian never developed the faith his wife possessed. He did become very friendly with the church and never opposed his children when they accepted their mother's religion. Later the family emigrated to the United States, and his oldest daughter became a missionary nurse to Ethiopia.

Yes, the Ashods were definitely happy now that they had "stayed by the stuff." They had taught the Biblical way of salvation to many people during those years: Emma Fruetiger,

Madame Story, Omirou, Konstantinides, Anesti, Kozma, Yaridians, Harantian, Cleanthi, Adolph, and the list went on. Soul-winning brought the Ashods happiness unlimited.

* Marie remained a staunch member until her death in 1962. She was working for a wealthy family in 1960 when one of the children became angry and pushed Marie down a marble staircase. She broke her leg and sustained internal injuries. The family took her to a hospital where they left her and never returned to get her. She never recovered fully from the accident and was finally transferred to a poor house. Istanbul Adventists visited her regularly until her death.

Chapter 7

BITTER DISAPPOINTMENT

The spring of 1925 brought great happiness to the Ashods. The orphanage, after being in Greece just two years, was being re-established in Turkey.

"Will I ever be glad to see those kids back," Aram said joyfully. "And, of course, the Aaron Larsons will be with them."

"And I'm real excited about that. We'll have mission workers with whom to share our experiences again!" Diamondola clasped her hands with pleasure.

If all of this was not enough to keep the Ashods stimulated, they were absolutely ecstatic when they got a letter from Despina saying, "Guess what? My son and I are coming to spend the summer with you in Turkey. I've been working on this surprise for six months, but the Turkish Consul here has given me all kinds of trouble. Even though I am married to an American citizen, Dr. Nazareth Crisp, and have been naturalized myself, my passport still shows that I was born in Turkey. The Turks are not interested in a former Christian citizen returning to Turkey. I told them I was just a harmless woman. At last they granted me a permit to enter Turkey. Praise the Lord. I can't wait to see you."

Diamondola could hardly contain herself after reading this welcome news. During the next few weeks, the Ashods and Theodora spent every spare minute planning for the momentous occasion.

"Be sure to pick the new grape leaves for my dolma," mother Theodora instructed Aram. "Then I must make Despina's favorite, baklava."

"We've got to make a picnic lunch and take them over to the island," Diamondola suggested, her eyes sparkling with anticipation.

"Ah, and the boy would certainly enjoy a day's boat trip up through the Bosphoros to the Black Sea," Aram added. "Do you suppose they have any such fancy mansions in California as there are along the shores of the Bosphoros?"

"They must. America is Utopia, isn't it?" Diamondola laughed.

They calcimined the bedroom walls and put newly starched sheets on the bed. They set their fancy pitcher and washbowl, a wedding gift, on the wash stand and hung a new towel on each end. The day Despina's ship was to arrive, they put fresh roses in a crystal vase and placed it on the dresser. Just before leaving for the docks, Diamondola took a last look about the guest room—everything was perfect. She thrilled with expectation as she closed the door and joined Aram and her mother to go down to the docks.

Meanwhile, Despina and her small son clung to the ship's rail, watching the skyline of Istanbul come into view. Despina trembled with emotion. It had been almost 10 years since she had last seen the faces of her loved one. Tears of joy streamed down her cheeks as she anticipated holding them close once more.

Down on the dock there was an equal amount of emotion brewing. Ashods and Theodora had arrived at the harbor early that morning. They watched eagerly as the ship pulled into harbor. Excitement escalated as they saw the anchor dropped, and the ship snubbed up to the dock. Then they saw the immigration officials mount the gang plank and board the ship. They waited impatiently for Despina to appear. After awhile a few passengers disembarked, met their families, and left the dock.

Ashods were alone on the peer; apprehension clouded their expectations.

"Where is Despina?" Diamondola asked anxiously as she shaded her eyes and scanned the deck for a glimpse of her sister.

"I can't understand this," Aram said as he nervously paced the dock. "There aren't many passengers coming to Turkey these days, so they should have had her papers processed long ago."

Then they caught a glimpse of Despina. They waved frantically to her. She waved back making some gestures that indicated there was a problem with the immigration officials. The Turkish consul in California had granted her a permit to enter the country, but not one to leave. Therefore, on the pretext that she did not have an exit visa, the officials would not allow her to leave the ship.

"Surely the immigration men won't be so mean as not to let Despina stay here with us this summer, would they?" Diamondola sobbed after learning of the impasse. "She's traveled halfway around the world to see us. Surely the knowledge of our long separation will melt their hearts, and they'll allow her to stay. It is only a small technicality on which they are holding her. It is within their power to change that in a minute. One press of the rubber stamp, and they could grant her an exit visa on the spot. Why are they so obstinate?"

Pleading, tears, bribes—nothing changed the minds of the officials. Even the fact that Despina wanted her mother to see her son, who had a congenital heart ailment which threatened his life, didn't phase the inhumane officials. It was almost with fiendish delight that these men inflicted this trauma upon the Ashods and Despina. The immigration officers folded their arms and smirked as they observed the tortured, desperate expressions written on the faces of the Ashod family. They kept Despina from the ship's rail, and Ashods off the gangplank in order that they might not even communicate with or see one another. The Ashods and Despina were trapped in a maddening situation that these diabolical men had the power to change.

Finally one official relented and allowed the Ashods and Theodora to go aboard ship to see Despina and her little boy. After only half an hour of hugs, tears, and kisses, however, the officials pulled the Ashods and Mrs. Keanides away from Despina's arms and pushed them down the gangplank. Despina had spent months planning this trip and four weeks on the ship for only a half hour reunion. Shortly thereafter, the ship sailed out of the harbor, taking a very despondent, brokenhearted Despina and son with it. Thus the day that had begun with such joyful anticipation ended in bitter disappointment.

Just before the family parted on the deck, they laid plans to meet in spite of the sadistic officials. Despina's boat would dock next in Greece. They decided that Despina should disembark there and go stay with Alexandra and Susanna. Diamondola and her mother would then go to Greece, and the family would have their reunion after all. This possibility assuaged the disappointment of not having Despina with them all summer.

From Greece Despina sent word that she had no problem getting both entrance and exit visas for that country, and that Diamondola and her mother should hurry to join the sisters. Diamondola and Theodora began working on their papers immediately. After weeks of delay, they finally got exit visas. Their ecstacy lasted only for a moment, however. In the next breath the officer, with steel glinting in his eye, said coldly, "But you, Diamondola Ashod, will not be permitted under any circumstances to return to Turkey."

After six months Diamondola and Theodora were forced to give up their plan of meeting the family in Greece. Despina's six-month visa for Greece expired, and she returned to the States. With resentment, they would always remember the summer of their shattered dreams.

"It's hard not to hate those men," Diamondola said through bitter tears. "We know the port officials could have given Despina clearance to leave the ship. We also know the government officials could have given mother and me permission to travel to Greece and back. Sometimes being a happy, contented ambassador to the Middle East is almost impossible. We may never get to see Despina in this world again—America is an ocean and a no-permit-to-travel away."

"It was very cruel and unjust of those men to do what they did," Aram agreed. "But there's coming a day when God will foil those men. They can never keep us apart eternally. So, until God directs otherwise, we'd better stay at our post of duty and accept bitter disappointments."

Chapter 8

AMBASSADORS GET A NEW ASSIGNMENT
(plus a new recruit)

Ashods tried to put the bitter disappointment of 1925 behind them and concentrate on more satisfying experiences. The first one came on the heels of the 1926 new year. After years of being in rented quarters, the General Conference of Seventh-day Adventists authorized the Turkish mission to purchase property. They found a suitable, three-story apartment building that could house two families and the mission offices. The mission president, Aaron Larson, moved into one apartment and the Ashods into the other. For the first time in their married lives, Ashods and mother Theodora Keanides had the privacy of their own place.

Satisfying as it was to have her own kitchen and living room, Diamondola was pleased with the mission house for another reason. She had been a part of the Adventist work in Turkey since 1907*, and never in her memory had the mission owned property in Istanbul. To her, the mission owning real estate in Istanbul was an omen of better times to come.

There remained one nagging problem. They still did not own a church, and their request to build one in the back garden of the mission property was refused. The Turkish government had not granted any permits to build Christian churches since 1913, and they had no intention of changing their minds. So, the Adventists were forced to continue to hold their Sabbath services in homes or in a rented Protestant church.

The Ashods work took on a routine—translating and publishing literature, doing the secretary and treasury work, and giving Bible studies. Though they seemed to work night and day, the membership did not grow in proportion to the hours of labor they expended. The newly baptized members only replaced the ones emigrating.

Mission presidents came and left—the Grins, the Larsons, the Backers. Ashods enjoyed them all even though their evening Bible work gave them little time to socialize. After a few years, Diamondola began to show signs of fatigue.

"Diamondola, I believe the years of incessant labor and stress are affecting your health," her mother said one morning at the breakfast table. "You look tired, and you aren't eating. I think you'd better go see Doctor Dinanian."

"So do I," Aram concurred. "And I shall take you there myself."

A few days later Diamondola was in Dr. Dinanian's office for a complete physical. After he completed his examination, he called the couple into his office for a consultation.

Aram was plainly worried. As he looked at Diamondola he thought to himself, "The strain of the years of working under most trying circumstances has taken its toll. She was never in robust health, but neither was she sickly. Maybe she has tuberculosis—she looks so pale and thin..."

"Well," the doctor said, seating himself. Aram sat bolt upright, clinging to the arms of his chair and almost dreading to hear the report. "Diamondola is about three months pregnant. She should feel more chipper in a month or so. Women usually feel better after they've passed the first trimester. I would advise her to get plenty of fresh air and exercise, rest when she's tired, and eat healthfully. Then I want to see Diamondola in another month to make sure she and the baby are both doing well."

"Ba-baby?" Aram stuttered rising from his chair. "Do you mean that Diamondola is going to have a BABY?"

51

The Doctor nodded. "Yes, pregnancies usually end with the birth of a baby."

"Bu-but that's imposs…, I mean, Diamondola and I have been married a number of years, and this is her first pregnancy. We're sort of old for…"

"Oh, I don't think Diamondola's too old to have a baby. Women her age bear healthy babies every day. You two have just reached the sensible age—the time in life when you'll make the best parents. I hope you're happy about this," the doctor smiled.

"Oh, I am! Believe me, I am!" Tears of happiness glistened in the father-to-be's eyes as he looked at his pregnant wife. He kissed her hand, "I've never been so touched or happy in my life. This is WONDERFUL!"

From that day forth, no expectant mother had more pampering than Diamondola received from her indulgent husband and mother.

The healthy baby daughter arrived on schedule. They named her Indra, the pen name of their friend, the late Diran Tcharakian. (The letters of the name, Diran, re-arranged form Indra.) Baby Indra was dedicated to God and the finishing of the work for which Tcharakian had been martyred.

Indra was a happy child and filled the home with sunshine. Diamondola only regretted that she could not spend all her time with the child for which she had secretly longed. The mission work still demanded much of her time. Fortunately, Grandmother Theodora lived in the home and was more than happy to take over the responsibility of caring for Indra.

They had barely made the adjustment to the new routine the baby imposed upon them when their lives took on a new twist. The Iran mission asked Aram to serve there as the Secretary-Treasurer. At last it was their turn to leave Turkey. They accepted the invitation and hoped that the journey would not be too arduous for their little mite and the delicate, 70-year old grandmother.

Aram arranged the transportation as best he could. There was no easy, direct route between Turkey and Iran. First, they took a boat going northeast through the Black Sea. They landed at Batum and caught a train which traveled through the Caucasus Mountains to Baku, a port city on the Caspian Sea. Next, they transferred their few belongings onto another boat going to the Persian town of Bandar-e Pahlavi. From there they rented a large taxi which took them to the mission headquarters in Teheran. Their journey had taken them hundreds of miles—from Paul's mission field in Asia Minor to the land of the Medes and Persians where Esther, Mordecai, and Daniel had served. The thought that they were walking in the footsteps of God's great heroes filled them with awe.

In Teheran, the Ashods Inc. set up housekeeping on the second floor of the mission house in a section that had been converted into an apartment. Elder F.F. Oster, the mission president, and his family lived on the first floor.

The first problem that confronted the Ashods was the water situation. The water flowed into the city from mountain springs and was carried through open gutters on either side of the streets to the residents. The Iranians squatted by the gutters and washed their clothes, dishes, and bodies in the water as it ran past their places. The mission, however, was allowed to divert the water from the gutter though a pipe into a reservoir in the basement of the mission house at night. After the dirt had settled, the water was drawn for household purposes. Diamondola could easily see that the water was too contaminated for human consumption.

One day she learned that the British Embassy had a daily supply of pure water. They ran a pipe from a mountain spring directly down to their compound. Diamondola made arrangements to purchase pure water from them. Every day an Iranian man came from the British Embassy with a barrel of pure water on a horsedrawn cart. He carried two buckets of the pure water upstairs to the Ashods' apartment, and dumped it into the kitchen storage tank. Diamondola was pleased that she had licked the drinking water problem. Then one day, to her horror, she looked out of the window and saw the water man giving his horse a drink in the pure water bucket! Worse yet, he had drawn the water from the gutter! From then on, she boiled all their drinking water. Further, she soaked their fruits and vegetables in permanganate solution, then rinsed them in boiled water. By taking these precautions, the Ashods avoided many of the diseases that others got from drinking impure water. Typhoid and dysentery were the most common killer diseases picked up in the polluted water.

The Ashods were drawn to the hard-working, friendly, and courteous Iranian people. They wanted to converse with them, but there was that language barrier.

Their first challenge was to learn Farsee, the common language of Iran. They engaged an educated young man who patiently taught them this refined, musical-sounding language. Study sessions became a form of recreation for them. Their teacher would sometimes quote poetry from two of the Persian masters, Saadi and Ferdowsi. Before two years had passed, the Ashods could converse comfortably with the Iranians. Aram even translated the Week of Prayer readings into Farsee. One day their teacher gave the Ashods a special thrill by inviting them to attend a session of the Iranian Parliament. He had a relative who was a member of this prestigious group. They were honored with seats reserved for the diplomatic corps. This was a real switch for the Ashods who had become accustomed to being treated like second-class citizens in Turkey.

Little Indra was learning languages too. She learned Turkish from her grandmother, English from her parents, Eastern Armenian from the church members, and Farsee from the neighborhood children and the servant Izmet.

Indra liked to chat with Izmet who had come into their lives rather unexpectedly. When Theodora found herself overwhelmed with the housework, laundry, caring for Indra, and cooking for guests, Ashods decided they should hire a servant to help her. They knew it would be difficult to find an honest woman, so they prayed about it. Within a few days Izmet, a Moslem lady, appeared at their door. She had neither references nor credentials, but she begged Diamondola to employ her. Diamondola's trained eye evaluated her critically. Izmet's appearance lacked appeal, but the desperate look in her eyes over-shadowed that objection.

"Look at me. I'm as healthy as I look. I can do any job you need. I don't lie or steal," Izmet assured Diamondola.

Diamondola hired Izmet in spite of her nagging doubts.

Indra tagged Izmet around the house. When she learned that Izmet did not know about Jesus, Indra discovered her mission field. She brought out her picture rolls and "preached sermons like Daddy" to Izmet. Actually, the servant was enthralled with the Bible stories. Who could tell them more clearly and appealingly than the three year old child? One day Indra presented a simple but most touching rendition of the story of Christ and the crucifixion. It left Izmet in tears. "I want a Savior like that, Baby Indra," she cried.

A few months later Diamondola learned that Izmet had not told the whole truth about her health. She suffered from the same affliction as the lady in Matthew 9:20. Unable to perform her tasks anymore, Izmet went AWOL. For several weeks the Ashods heard nothing from her. They were concerned for this woman whom they believed God had sent to them for some reason. Diamondola continually enquired about Izmet's whereabouts. She finally found her in a state hospital in Teheran. She had undergone surgery, infection had set in, and her wound was not healing. Diamondola went to Izmet's side to encourage the suffering woman. She gave Izmet an adult version of the story of Jesus, told her how much He loved her, and that He could heal her. Even in her agony, Izmet reached out for truth and hope. "I want Jesus more than I want healing," the suffering woman murmured. "Will He take women to heaven?"

"Yes, He will. Everyone is equal in His sight," Diamondola assured her wiping the feverish brow. Diamondola knew this thought was novel to Izmet's Moslem thinking.

A week later, Miss Nanajan went to the hospital with Diamondola to see Izmet. The doctor told them that peritonitis had spread to such an extent that Izmet's case was hopeless unless they did another surgery. That procedure was not feasible because Izmet was too weak. When Diamondola and Miss Nanajan talked to Izmet about the miracle Jesus performed for the woman with the issue of blood, Izmet stirred slightly and gasped, "Pray for me. I be - lieve."

The two ladies took Izmet's clammy hand in theirs and prayed for God to heal the patient, if it was His will and to His glory.

The next time Diamondola neared the hospital it was with a degree of apprehension. To her surprise, she found Izmet sitting up in bed, quite alive and well. "Oh, Mistress, Jesus has healed me just like the woman in the story. The morning after you prayed, my fever and infection left me, and there was no need for a second surgery," Izmet said, giving a testimony of the power of Jesus to everyone in the ward.

Then the Moslem nurse called the attention of everyone in the ward to Diamondola. "See this Christian lady?" she asked, obviously impressed. "She comes faithfully to see her Moslem servant and prays for her. God answers her prayers and Izmet is healed. Do we Moslems do as much for others?" She then invited Diamondola to pray for the other patients in the ward.

Izmet was never able to return to her household tasks, but she remained a devoted friend. The seed that was planted by the young recruit, Indra, eventually grew, and Izmet was harvested for the kingdom of God.

* Diamondola began her mission service when she was only 13. She traveled extensively with Elder AcMoody as his translator.

56

* * * *

The reader should bear in mind that conditions that existed in Teheran 50 years ago, are not necessarily the same today. Every country has made its advances.

Chapter 9

"HERE I AM LORD—BUT PLEASE DON'T SEND ME ON AN IRANIAN BUS"

The Adventist work in Iran had been established by pioneer missionaries F. F. Oster and Henry Dirksen. (See *To Persia With Love* by Kenneth Oster.) In the 1920's the work was further bolstered by the medical clinics of Doctors Arzoo and Hargreaves, and seven schools scattered throughout the country. Before the Ashods arrived, however, most of the schools had been forced to close, but the churches and clinics in this vast territory (636,293 square miles) were still functioning.

Aram, as mission treasurer, was asked to travel to these outposts to check accounts and audit the books. The innocent man eagerly anticipated this assignment—he would get to travel and see the beautiful sites of Iran. Aram had no idea what he was in for, but on the first trip he found out.

An hour out of Teheran they hit the first of the bone-shattering, rutted roads with holes so deep the bus could lose a wheel in them. Aram held onto the bench seat in front of him to try to ease some of the jolts. He hoped his brains wouldn't slip down into his feet before he reached his destination. He supposed his spine had suffered irreparable damage; he knew his clothes had. His jacket wore thin across the shoulders where he was constantly bouncing off the hard back of his seat. There was basically no padding on the seat, either. Within two hours after the journey began, Aram had lost all enthusiasm for travel on Iranian buses.

Aram looked forward to the end of each day's travel. When the bus stopped for the night, he would search for an inn that had a Turkish bath, then drop his satchel and brief case in the room, and run to soak his bruised and aching body in the warm water. The inns themselves were a health hazard. Upon entering the room, Aram would go to the bed, lift the sheet, pick the bedbugs off one side of the mattress, throw them on the terrazzo floor and tramp on them. Then he'd turn the mattress over and repeat the process. He never got them all, however, and the escapees' bites kept him busy scratching the next day. Lice were another aggravating menace. Since bedding was washed infrequently, Aram's body could easily pick up the nits from the former occupant of the sheets. "Cooties" also migrated from one passenger to another on the bus.

Aram had to take his food and drinking water with him on these out-of-town excursions. His sanitized digestive system could not tolerate the food served at the roadside cafes. He appreciated the rest stops because it gave him a respite from the jostling bus. Whenever he reached his destination, he felt about three inches shorter. Like an honest measure he was "pressed down and shaken together."

Traveling held other hazards as well. The poorly constructed roads were more dangerous in bad weather. Ruts became so deep that the bus would hit high center, and the wheels would lose traction. Sharp stones slashed tires and tore open oil pans. Brakes burned out on steep inclines, and run-away vehicles careened off the cliffs or crashed into the mountains. Much time was wasted making bus and tire repairs. Opium smugglers caused other delays. Buses were frequently stopped by police who set up road blocks to catch the traffickers. Opium addicts, losing track of time in their euphoria, stretched out the rest periods at the bus stops until they finished their smoke.

Vehicle accidents were all too common. Just how many times Aram miraculously escaped injury he will never know, but there was one experience he will always remember. He deliberately scheduled a trip with a certain bus driver. He even gave the man a tip to save the seat opposite himself. Aram preferred that spot because the seat was usually cleaner and further from the opium smokers. When the time for departure came, Aram boarded the bus only to find that his seat was occupied by another man. There were no empty seats on the bus, so Aram returned home, rather upset by the delay of several hours. He found space on the next bus and was off for his destination. On the way they caught up with the first bus. What a pitiful sight! The bus had overturned, injuring most of the passengers. The man who sat in the seat for which Aram had bargained was killed.

Another time Aram was traveling in the mountains in rainy weather, a trip everyone in their right mind should avoid. There were no rails on the edge of the precipices to keep the vehicles from sliding off the steep embankments to the valley below. The road led through a deep canyon and clung precariously to the edge of a rocky mountain. The bus slid in the mud, slipped off the road, but, fortunately, tipped against the mountain side. Aram was not even shaken from his seat, but another man, who had his arm out the window, had his elbow crushed. In his misery he told Aram, "I knew I shouldn't have come on this trip. I sneezed once before boarding the bus, and everyone knows that is bad luck." Aram had not known this valuable information, but now he was educated.

Fortunately Aram shared this interesting trivia with Diamondola. Sometime later the Ashods were both asked to attend a workers' meeting outside of Teheran. They engaged a taxi to take them to their destination. As the driver was tying their suitcases on top of the car, Diamondola sneezed once. The taxi driver stopped his work and looked alarmed. Then Diamondola, remembering one sneeze was a bad omen, faked a second sneeze. The taxi driver heaved a sigh of relief and returned to his work. They made the trip safely.

When Aram wasn't traveling, he spent a lot of time trying to get their mission and hospital supplies released from the customs house. He enjoyed those days about as much as a good case of the bubonic plague. Delay was the name of the game, and the officials apparently vied with one another to concoct excuses for the endless delays. "Add to your faith, patience," Aram told himself as he bit his tongue. In the end, he always succeeded in getting the goods released, but not until his nerves seemed shredded.

Aram and Diamondola enjoyed their translation work. Aram translated the Sabbath School lessons, Week of Prayer Readings, a new health book, *How to Meet the Epidemics*, and other literature. Besides their Bible classes, they trained five students chosen from the schools to become workers. During one two-year period Aram had to spend most of his time in Tabriz, Iran, helping Elder Tulazevsky with evangelism. He made frequent trips home to see his little Indra and her mother. But alas, the journey always had to be made on an Iranian bus!

Chapter 10

THE MK'S or the MISSIONARIES' KIDS

Aram left his office and went down to the mission compound's garden where his Little Darling was watching the Oster boys play. He scooped Indra into his arms and kissed her chubby little cheek. "How's daddy's big girl today?"

"I'm not big like the boys," she said longingly.

"You'll get bigger, and you'll get older, don't worry," Aram assured her. As he "horsied" her up the steps to their apartment, Indra clung to his back, squealing delightedly.

"What you got to feed a hungry pair for supper?" Aram asked as he burst into the kitchen, depositing Indra on the floor.

"Eggplant, greens, cucumbers, tomatoes, rice, and melon," Theodora answered.

"Sounds good, doesn't it, Indra? Now run and wash your hands." Aram turned to Diamondola who was working on some correspondence lessons from the Home Commission of the General Conference. "She's such fun. She's our heritage from the Lord."

"Yes, she is," Diamondola responded. "I don't know what I'd do without her. I wish we could have at least one more child. What if something should happen to Indra?"

"Hush, my dear! Don't even think about it," Aram admonished. "Let's concentrate on raising our Little Blessing to love and serve the Lord."

"I am. Mother and I both teach her as much of the Bible as her little mind can absorb."

"That you do," agreed Aram.

"Have you noticed that Indra has a penchant for any kind of creature?" Diamondola asked her husband. "Maybe she'll be a biologist. She spends hours playing with the slimy tadpoles or watching the ants, but her all-time favorite is her cat. When the census was taken today, she insisted that the officer record the name of her cat with the rest of the family. She made a hammock for the cat and sang 'Jesus songs' to it as she swung it back and forth. She dressed it in doll clothes and took its temperature 'under its arm.' I had to stop her from giving the cat an enema in it's ear. She even worries that the cat will never make it to heaven because she can't get it to pray."

"She's a fun child," Aram commented as he laughed over her antics.

Time passed quickly in Iran. The Oster and Ashod families grew closer as they shared many happy experiences. The large garden on the compound with its pond, big trees, and flowers was like a retreat for the mission families in the midst of a large, bustling city. The Oster boys, who were much older than Indra, thoroughly enjoyed the garden where they spent endless hours playing with their friends. They were kindly tolerant of Indra, who must have been a nuisance to them occasionally. One day, however, the boys really appreciated having Indra around. Kenneth and Francis had climbed a large tree, then scooted from the limbs onto a portion of an old building. Before long they realized that they couldn't get back down the way they had come up. Not knowing what else to do, they called Indra and told her to go tell their parents to bring a ladder so they could climb down.

Even though Indra was quite young, she sensed the urgency of the situation. She ran to the office where she found the adults in a committee meeting. Indra was very excited and stuttered out her message. No one caught it. Indra's parents were slightly embarrassed by her interruption and did not want her to get the idea that she could burst into the office whenever it struck her fancy. Although she never had done this before, they were determined not to indulge her whims. Subsequently, she was ushered to the door and told to go play.

Indra rushed back to the boys. "They won't believe me and come help you. But don't worry. If you should die up there, Jesus will find you, resurrect you, and take you to heaven." Then remembering that the boys seldom wore their halos straight she added, "Maybe."

"Fine comfort she is," groaned Ken beginning to feel desperate. "Indra, please go talk to them again." Then turning to Francis he said, "Do you realize we're trusting our lives to that little kid? What if no one listens to her?"

Indra sped back to the office. With tears in her eyes she burst in upon the meeting crying loudly, "Come quickly before they die."

This brought the whole committee as one man to their feet. "DIE? WHO? WHERE?" they asked anxiously. Then they followed Indra to the emergency site.

They put up a ladder, and the boys climbed down to terra firma. Father Oster gave the adventurers some advice about exploring forbidden territory.

During the summer months, Teheran became very hot. In order to sleep comfortably, people moved their beds into their gardens or onto the flat roofs of their houses. The Osters and Ashods slept in the mission garden. However, they had to sleep under cheesecloth netting because the miserable sandflies were so small they could slip right through the regular mosquito nets.

One morning Diamondola opened her eyes and thought she was hallucinating. She sat up abruptly and quietly awakened the rest of the mission family. "Look up in that tree," she said pointing. "Do I see a live monkey swinging on a limb, or have I taken leave of my senses?"

The Oster boys were ecstatic. They coaxed the monkey onto the porch with some peanuts. Then they tempted him into the hallway, and pronto! They closed the door, and the monkey was their pet. Their joy was short lived, however, for soon the servant of the doctor who lived near the mission compound came to claim the monkey. Ken and Francis were disappointed to lose their pet. They had fallen in love with him. When the doctor learned how anxious the boys were to keep the monkey, he gladly rid himself of the pest.

Shangouly, as the monkey was named, was a source of amusement to the boys. Diamondola noticed, however, that Shangouly seemed to have a dislike for Indra and bared his teeth every time she came near. The Ashods feared that one day Shangouly would break loose from his chain and attack Indra. But Ken was the victim. Shangouly bit him on the leg, leaving a bad wound. Elder Oster, who had never been too thrilled with the nuisance anyway, took Shangouly back to his former owner.

Sometime later, the Ashods saw Shangouly with a little gypsy boy. He was dressed in a red outfit and did tricks to earn coins for his master. Diamondola couldn't resist the temptation to give him a little pat on his back, but was glad he was gone from the compound.

"Shangouly won't go to heaven because he gets mean," Indra observed. "The animals in heaven will be gentle, and the camel will kiss Jesus."

"The camel will kiss Jesus? Strange idea," Diamondola thought. "But missionaries' kids growing up in the Middle East where camels are so prevalent think like other kids growing up in this environment. Which proves, 'MK's' are just ordinary kids."

Chapter 11

SANDFLIES, SPOTS, AND SELJUK

Indra had been a fairly healthy child all her life, but one morning Diamondola noticed Indra touching four small red spots on her nose. There was another one directly under her eye, right at the base of the eyelid. A few days later when the red, raised spots had not disappeared, the parents took her to the Institute of Pasteur in Teheran for a check-up. The doctor took some tests and confirmed their worst fears. The wicked little sandfly that carries the causative organism of the Oriental sore had chosen Indra for its victim and her face as the place of infestation.

Dr. Kerandel, the director for the Institute of Pasteur, responded to their anxious query, "Yes, Indra is in grave danger of losing her eye. If you want to try to save her eye, and maybe even her life, you need to go to Dr. Habib Adel, a specialist, for immediate treatment. You realize that she has been infested in the danger triangle—the area around her nose where the infection sometimes moves on into the brain.

The Oriental sore, or Cutaneous Leishmaniasis, was quite common in Iran in those days. It starts as a small, reddish, itchy spot on some exposed area of the skin. It then enlarges and becomes a bloody, discharging ulcer. The discharge dries and forms a crust, then the ulcer discharges again and again, slowly getting larger. The sore may become as large as a half dollar. Healing is very slow, taking a year or more. And when it is healed, it leaves deep, sometimes disfiguring, ugly scars.

With heavy hearts, the Ashods took their darling to Dr. Adel. He gave them a ray of hope. "The laboratory has developed an injection that seems to help most patients. Come back tomorrow, and I will have some serum ready to start treatments on Indra."

The next day the Ashods returned to Dr. Adel's office with Indra. The serum had to be injected in small amounts directly into the raised red spots of the sore. Indra was not prepared for this. When the Doctor came to her with the needle, she struggled to free herself. After numerous attempts, the doctor finally said that he had lost too much of the serum and would have to prepare a fresh batch. He told them to return in two days, and he would have more serum prepared and a couple of assistants on hand to restrain the child.

Diamondola spent the next two days preparing Indra for her ordeal. She tried to explain the medical procedures. "It is very important that you lie still and let the doctor inject the serum. Then Jesus will help the sores go away without leaving ugly scars or causing blindness in your eye. We must do our part and cooperate, Darling."

Indra listened carefully, but Diamondola was not certain just how much she had gotten across to her.

The dreaded day came. Indra was very quiet as they took her to the clinic.

The doctor asked Aram to attend his daughter; Diamondola remained in the waiting room. There she listened and prayed. Not a sound came from the office area, and Diamondola began to worry about the phenomenon. Presently the child and her father appeared.

"I am so proud of Indra, Mommy," Aram said. "She didn't need anyone to hold her. She lay as still as a little mouse and didn't utter one peep when the doctor injected the five spots. She didn't even wince when the needle went through the skin to the other side. She really deserves the chocolate candy bar we promised her as a reward for cooperating with the doctor."

Aram confided to Diamondola privately, "I was amazed at the child's self control. My heart ached as I saw tears rise to the surface and course down her little cheeks as she lay on the table."

Diamondola hugged and kissed her little one. "Honey, I'm glad you were so brave. Let's go get that candy bar."

Out on the street, Indra skipped along between them, holding their hands. "It wasn't very easy, Mommy, 'cause Satan told me to kick and scream. Then I heard Jesus say, 'Lie still and quiet, and I will help you.' So I obeyed Jesus."

The parents praised the Lord for the trusting relationship their child had developed with Jesus.

Indra's sores developed and followed the usual pattern—bleeding, discharging, and crusting. This continued for a whole year. A large scab formed, covering her entire nose. Finally the doctor said it was time to remove the scab. Underneath it was the reddest, rawest-looking nose one could ever imagine, but gradually the sore healed leaving only four small, pock-like marks. In a few years those too disappeared. The Lord had answered their prayers.

Though it seemed impossible to the Ashods, Indra was five and ready for kindergarten. They sent her to the Calvert School, an American institution for foreign children in Teheran. The year went well until one day when Indra came home from school with a fever.

Diamondola read the note the headmistress had sent home with Indra. She laughed and commented, "Looks like the Turks are still out to get us. The headmistress says that Indra probably has the whooping cough. She got it from Seljuk, the son of the Turkish Ambassador."

Theodora stiffened with alarm.

"Oh, relax, mother," Diamondola said patting her. "Indra just has a childhood disease. I'm only joking about the Turks. Seljuk just happened to be the first child in school to catch whooping cough."

Diamondola and Theodora took every precaution possible with Indra, but she seemed to get worse each day. Indra whooped, coughed, and vomited until there was practically nothing left of her but a thin little skeleton. The doctor told them that he could do nothing more for her. What should have been a simple disease turned into a life-threatening situation. The parents prayed fervently for God to spare her life.

Summer arrived. The doctor advised the Ashods to get Indra out of the heat, turmoil, and dust of the city. They knew the advise was good. Indra, in her weakened condition, would be especially susceptible to tuberculosis, dysentery, and other common summer diseases. They discussed several possibilities. Summer resorts were out of the question; they could not afford them. But, as usual, God, who is never late but seldom early, had an answer to their prayers just waiting in the wings. Just when their frustrations had peaked, God sent the Zees to them.

Chapter 12

AT GENERAL ZEE'S

"He who loves purity of heart, and whose speech is gracious, will have the king as his friend." Proverbs 22:11 is a nice scripture, but how many people see a fulfillment of it? The Ashods came close to having such an experience.

A few months before Indra's illness, the Ashods had come in contact with a prestigious Russian lady who had been married to the Iranian Ambassador to Monaco, Prince Zee. Upon the death of her husband, Mrs. Zee returned to Teheran to live with her son, General Zee, and his English wife.

One day the older Madame Zee* sent her shoes out to be repaired. When the servant returned with the mended shoes, Madame Zee found a handbill announcing some Adventist meetings in her package. This captured her interest immediately because she had learned of Adventism when she was a young girl back in Russia. She was thrilled to learn that there were Adventists in Teheran, so she made her way to their meetings. The Ashods did not know that she was from elite society when they invited her to their simple home for dinner. Soon a strong bond of friendship developed. It was not until the Ashods were invited to the Zees' mansion that they discovered they had befriended someone from Iran's upper echelon.

"Well, if we can't be a friend to the king or shah, we'll just have to settle for the next in line," Diamondola laughed.

"They need true friends too. We can fill that need," Aram suggested.

"Right. Besides, I like her very much. She never puts on airs or makes me feel inferior. She's just a nice lady," Diamondola added.

One day when the Ashods had Indra with them, they met the young Mrs. Zee. She introduced her daughter Leila to Indra. The girls were about the same age and, like two magnets, were immediately drawn to each other. Thereafter, the parents brought the two girls together as often as possible to play.

When Mrs. Zee learned that Indra's whooping cough had ended in a physically debilitating condition, she was deeply concerned. The same afternoon that the doctor suggested a drier, cooler climate for Indra, young Mrs. Zee called on the Ashods. "I believe that breathing the purer country air would help your daughter recover her health. I've come especially to invite you folks to spend the summer with us on our estate at Larak. The girls will love being together, and you'll enjoy the invigorating mountain atmosphere too. Please accept my invitation," she urged pleasantly.

Diamondola was speechless. God had impressed this lady to provide for their needs before they even had time to ask Him. As yet, no one but God knew about the doctor's recommendation. They accepted the gracious invitation, and Aram moved his family up to the Zee estate; he would join them on weekends.

General Zee's Larak estate was an oasis of Edenic beauty located at the base of a mountain. A stream, emanating from a gurgling spring, flowed through the middle of the immense walled property. Within the walls, a variety of fruit trees groaned under the burden of their delectable, juicy product; well-kept gardens produced an abundance of choice vegetables; flowers bloomed everywhere. Lovely, big shade trees, embracing at the tops, lined the walks. As the Ashods walked down the path with the evening sun splashing gold and crimson across the western sky, they felt they had entered God's cathedral.

In this paradise there was a large house for the Zees and a small, very comfortable guest house for the Ashods. At night, they fell asleep with the sound of the water falls and the bubbling brook; in the morning, they awakened to the lilting songs of the birds; during the day, they ate from the estate's bounty—fresh vegetables, pears, peaches, apricots, apples, mulberries, and plums. General Zee loved animals. There was a baby bear chained in one corner of the garden. Cats, dogs, porcupines, snakes, and jackals roamed freely about his property.

Jackals, the Ashods were soon to learn, could push their freedom too far. For some time stockings, shoes, and under garments were disappearing at night while they slept. This perplexed them since they knew that the Larak staff was honest to the core. Then, one day a ruckus in the cellar caused them to call the gardener. He caught their thief red-handed (or red-pawed). He found the jackal trying to stash away the items he had absconded from the Ashods at night by stealthily entering through their open, screenless window.

Perhaps the favorite pet on the estate was the Indian mongoose named Rikki Tikki Tavi, after the mongoose character in Rudyard Kipling's JUNGLE BOOK. The people of Larak often met this officious little creature snooping about the property making everyone's business his own. Rikki Tikki seemed to believe that he was indispensable since he could kill poisonous snakes much larger than himself.

Once a week Diamondola went to town to purchase groceries. She kept the food in a screened-in cupboard outside on the shady side of the house. She put the eggs in a wire basket and hung it in the bedroom window. She noticed that their egg supply was dwindling more rapidly than what they ate. Then one morning she heard a sound at the window. She lay still and watched as Rikki Tikki latched onto the basket, drew himself over the edge, and bit into an egg just hard enough to get his teeth into the shell, but not hard enough to break it. He then carried the egg to his lair, never waiting to pick up buttered toast to complete his menu.

Later that day, Diamondola and Indra met Rikki Tikki in the garden and offered him an egg. He haughtily refused their generosity—eggs were a breakfast item, and then, only if he could steal them.

Outside of the walled estate, General Zee grew acres of wheat. Indra and Leila liked to watch the men harvest and thresh the grain. The workers did it just like it had been done in Bible times. The men cut the wheat with a sickle, gathered it into sheaves, then piled it in a large circle on the threshing floor. When the kernels were dry and firm, oxen were hitched to a threshing board that had flint stones driven into the bottom of it. Then the oxen were driven around and around on top of the grain. The stones cut the stems of wheat into short straws and shook loose the kernels of wheat. The old man driving the oxen would often let the girls ride around on the threshing board.

Next Leila and Indra watched the men winnow the grain. They tossed the straw into the air with wooden forks. The wind blew the light chaff into a pile off to the side; the heavier grain kernels fell directly down onto the canvass. At Zee's place the ox that trod out the wheat was not muzzled, and the old servant made sure that the other creatures of the field got their share of the wheat too. He would throw a handful of new grain into the air saying, "For the birds." He'd scoop up a second handful and scatter it saying, "For the ants." The third handful he threw was "For the poor." Indra would never forget the object lesson the old man taught them—all God's creatures and people should be generously cared for by those who have been abundantly blessed.

By the end of the summer, Indra had gained weight and was radiantly healthy. All traces of her illnesses had disappeared. Ashods thanked the Zees and God for providing for their physical necessities and their sensory pleasures.

*Madame Zee became a Seventh-day Adventist. Though General Zee was a Moslem, he never opposed his mother's religion. He was always a loving son. His kindness extended to her friends as well. Once when he accompanied the Shah on a visit to Turkey, he brought the Ashods back some Turkish Delight (Turkey's special jellied candy filled with nuts). When Madame Zee died sometime later, the Ashods explained the state of the dead to the young Mrs. Zee, a nominal Christian. The General, being a Moslem, already believed in the resurrection of the dead. The Zees were satisfied that their mother would see God one day and be reunited with her friends, the Ashods.

Chapter 13

THE BRIDE FROM ISTANBUL

Diamondola always looked forward to mail time. Letters kept her in contact with old friends. This day she was especially pleased to find a letter from Kristin, a young friend from Istanbul. Kristin had enclosed a photograph of herself which Diamondola studied lovingly before setting it on the mantle. Then she devoured the contents of the letter. Toward the end there was a sad note: "Mother is sick and cannot work anymore. We are living together in one room. I am working in different homes trying to earn enough to support us and pay her medical bills."

"Trouble! That is the story of Kristin's life," observed Theodora who listened as Diamondola read the letter aloud. "I wonder if Kristin and her mother will always be plagued by tragedies. How I wish they could have a reversal of fortune."

"So do I," agreed Diamondola. "Kristin's morning for joy is past due."

"I should guess so," added Theodora as she threw her dishtowel on the counter and sat down across the table from her daughter. "I was just recalling some of her adversities. First, her father died when she very young. Then, her mother took the four children to Istanbul and slaved away at menial jobs to put food on the table. After the two middle ones married and left home, Eli, the oldest brother, went to Germany, worked in a leather factory, and sent money home to Kristin and her mother. Those were the good days."

"Yes," sighed Diamondola. "Then Eli went to Yugoslavia, started his own leather factory, and built a house on the property for himself, Kristin, and their mother. But before they could join him, he was stabbed to death in his house by thieves. And to think, Kristin and her mother would never have known what happened to Eli if they had not read about his murder in the Turkish newspaper."

"Terrible!" Theodora commented. "But it was at this low-tide juncture in their lives that Kristin and her mother came to us at the mission in Istanbul. You found work for her as a governess. She became an Adventist and fell in love with a young man."

"What a disappointment that turned out to be!" A frown creased Diamondola's forehead. "She and I had had such fun preparing her wedding dress and trousseau. Then her fiancee broke off the engagement. We wept together as we packed her things away. She was still recovering from her disappointment when we got our call to Iran. As we left Turkey, her mother extracted a promise from me, 'Please don't forget Kristin. If anything happens to me, take her over to Iran to live with you.' Now that her mother is ill, we may be sending for her any day. I'd love to see her again. She has the qualities of a princess but is relegated to servitude for sheer existence. If it weren't for bad luck, Kristin would have no luck at all."

Diamondola looked at the letter in her hand and wondered how, if ever, Kristin's fortune would change. Although no one knew it then, God was already working on a change of venue for the young lady.

A few weeks after this scenario took place, Mrs. Shirvanian from Isfahan called on Diamondola. She asked if she could stay with the Ashods while her husband, Pastor Shirvanian, had surgery for his ulcers at the American Hospital in Teheran. Knowing what it would mean to Vagarshak to have his wife near him during the ordeal, the Ashods gladly invited her into their home.

One day Mrs. Shirvanian noticed the picture of Kristin on Ashods' mantle.

"Who is this beautiful, refined-looking girl?" she asked examining the photo.

"Oh, that's Kristin, a dear friend in Istanbul," Diamondola answered.

"Married?"

"No, but deserving," Diamondola answered.

"Hmmm!" said the lady, squinting her eyes while her brain spun ideas. "I just might play matchmaker. We have a wealthy family in Isfahan who have four sons. All of them are married except the youngest one, Joseph. Let me assure you, it is with great determination that he has remained a bachelor. Many families have wanted him to marry their daughters. But Joseph wants an Adventist girl, and he says he would be partial to one from a foreign country. Now doesn't Kristin fit into that category? May I take this picture to Isfahan to show him?"

Diamondola readily agreed to be inducted into the clandestine scheme, and secretly prayed that it would result in marriage for Kristin and Joseph. She wanted to tell the pastor how happy she was that his ulcers might mean a new life for Kristin, but she discreetly refrained from saying so.

When the photo was presented to Joseph, he studied it carefully and prayed about Kristin. He felt impressed that this might be his girl, so he went to Teheran to learn more about her from the Ashods. They gave him an honest, glowing report and supplied him with her address.

For the next two years Joseph and Kristin corresponded. Joseph was satisfied that Kristin was his love, but before he officially proposed, he felt it was only fair to explain to her his family's background. They were metal craftsmen, descendants from Caucasians who once lived within the Russian border. Their patriarchal family of artisans were a proud people who remained exclusive.

77

They were suspicious of strangers and didn't want foreigners in the family—this was a barrier the couple would have to work through. But Kristin was used to surmounting obstacles, so she agreed to become Joseph's wife. When her mother died, there was nothing to keep her in Turkey any longer.

When Joseph informed his family that he was bringing a bride for himself from Istanbul, he was about as popular as the chicken-pox. Those rating second in the Gabriel family's book of persona non-grata were the pastor, Mrs. Shirvanian, who had conjured up the matrimony idea, and the Ashods of Teheran. Joseph himself was now a fledgling pastor for the Adventist church. The clan forgave him this departure from family tradition of becoming a metal craftsman, but to pay to bring a bride from Istanbul? This was intolerable. So wheels were set in motion to cool Cupid's heels. In the meantime, Kristin arrived in Teheran.

One morning a prestigious appearing man presented himself at the Teheran mission and asked to be directed to Ashods' house. Aram greeted the stranger warmly and seated him in the parlor. They had no idea who the stranger was, but tried to engage him in conversation to learn more about him. The man courteously maintained his reserve and concealed his identity. They discussed different subjects casually, and the Ashods discovered that the man was educated and well informed. Their years of living in Turkey had taught the Ashods to guard their conversation. So far they hoped they had done this.

"Ah, refreshments," Diamondola thought. "It is the Abrahamic custom here in the Middle East to offer food to strangers. This will stall for time, and maybe then he will reveal his identity."

Now Kristin, being the youngest girl of marriageable age in the household, was called to do the honors. Ashods noted that from the moment Kristin entered the room the man's eyes were fixed upon her. When she left with the tray of dirty dishes he asked, "Is this the bride from Istanbul?" The Ashods assured him that she was. Then he told them that he was the relative of

Joseph's who had been delegated by the family to investigate if the girl was "right".

The conversation then became more cordial but still guarded. He accepted the Ashods' dinner invitation. At the table, he continued to eye Kristin and question her. Kristin was aware of the stranger's extraordinary interest in her. Soon she suspected that he was sent by Joseph's family to evaluate her; very cleverly she concealed her suspicions from him. She parleyed his questions expertly and gained his respect. Before he left he said with a chuckle, "I'm going back and tell the family that the bride from Istanbul is not only worthy of Joseph, but maybe too good for him. That should straighten out their kink of prejudice."

Kristin's night of weeping was over, and her morning of joy had come. Now she and Diamondola could settle down to making final plans for the wedding.

Chapter 14

HOUSE OF REFUGE

For as long as Diamondola could remember, she had either lived in or run a house of refuge. Her childhood home in Brousa had been a refuge for the Protestant and Adventist ministers, and anyone else who needed shelter. The Rumeli Hissar house in Istanbul was rented for the sole purpose of caring for the refugees and orphans. Since their marriage, it seemed that almost always someone needed asylum in Ashods' home. They were enjoying Kristin, but another, more desperate refugee was about to join them.

One Sabbath in church Diamondola was astonished to see Hosanna, a church member she had last seen in Turkey as an exile on the death march into the Syrian Desert. During those days of Christian persecution, Diamondola and the mission president had traveled into the interior to give blankets, food, and clothing to the helpless Armenian refugees. The relief was only temporary, however; the Christians who did not freeze or starve to death on the way, were sometimes executed by the Turkish soldiers.

Diamondola and Hosanna clasped each other in a tight embrace while tears of joy coursed down their cheeks. "Whatever brings you to Teheran?" Diamondola managed to ask. "I never thought I'd see you alive again on this earth."

"I know. I don't allow myself to think of those days of horror. I was all but dead when some Christian Arabs kidnapped me. Two

80

weeks later they smuggled me into the Armenian section of Beirut. There I became a rug weaver. Soon I met Haroun Kedarian. His wife died during the deportation, but he and the boys escaped from their captors and made it to Beirut. He became a carpenter, and we married. Between the two of us we were able to make a decent living. Haroun's oldest boy married and moved to Teheran. He owns a small business here. He invited his father, teenage brother, and me to join him. Haroun decided it would be nice for all of us to live together again, so we withdrew our savings, bought traveler's checks and bank notes, and moved here."

The next few weeks the Kedarians spent every Sabbath with the Ashods. They were handicapped in that they couldn't speak Farsee, the language of Iran. The Kedarians could communicate only with the people who spoke Turkish and Armenian. Still, they were happy—at first. As the weeks passed, however, the Kedarians became withdrawn and despondent. The Ashods finally persuaded them to share their problem.

First of all, the young Kedarians were not Adventists, and they made this a point of contention. Furthermore, it became evident that the purpose of the oldest son in bringing his parents to Iran was to get their money. The Kedarians had been in his home only a few weeks when the oldest son asked for, then demanded, that his father turn over ALL of his savings to him. With the money the son intended to purchase a bigger business, but he would not make the parents or younger brother partners with him or allow them to receive any return on their investment. When the wicked son's demands were not met, he and his wife became surly and despotic with the parents. After a few months of harassment, the Adventist Kedarians went to the Ashods in their distress.

"My son has brought us here to rob us of our savings," said Mr. Kedarian, tears welling up in his eyes. "He and his wife are harsh and cruel to us. They beat and starve us because we do not give them our money. If we give them our money, I know they will put us out on the street."

"You'll never need to live out on the street as long as you have your church family here," Diamondola assured him, patting his arm.

"God bless you, sister," he said, brushing away a tear with his calloused hand. "I am so hurt! I can't trust my own flesh and blood! I never expected my son to be my persecutor. I love him. I want him saved."

A few days later, Mr. Kedarian died of a heart attack. (Or was it a broken heart? Or had they poisoned his food?) As soon as the body was in the grave, the oldest son came to his step-mother demanding that she turn over "his father's savings" immediately.

"But half of the money is mine. I earned it weaving rugs," Hosanna protested.

Cold steel glinted in the oldest son's eyes as he swore, "I'll get that money by hook or by crook and leave you and my brother destitute."

Hosanna secretly slipped from the house one day with her assets in tow and fled to the Ashods. Since Aram was away on mission business at the time, Diamondola persuaded Elder Oster to help her save Hosanna from being swindled. Oster took all of the bank drafts and traveler's checks and put them in the mission safe until legalities could be worked out.

Hosanna contacted the oldest boy and proposed that she would give him half of his father's share of the money, even though he had not helped in any way to earn the money. The rest of the money she would keep for herself and the younger, more worthy stepson. But the eldest son was infuriated with her offer and threatened everyone who aided Hosanna. Therefore, since Elder Oster did not think it was wise for the mission to be the depositor of the disputed monies, he transferred them to a bank.

Back home, the wicked son and his wife contrived new forms of persecution for Hosanna and the younger boy. Besides starving and beating them, they held them hostage in a locked room. Even though they were carefully policed, the good son managed to escape through a very small window and flee to Beirut. Before he left, he told his step-mother to follow him to Beirut where he would care for her. Hosanna knew escape for her was impossible—she was older, a woman, and could not stand the rigors of a thousand mile flight. Her freedom was contingent upon her handing over the money. But even if she gave the greedy couple the money, would they release her? As a hostage, she wasn't allowed to go out of the room or to contact anyone.

Meanwhile, the wicked son,"by hook or by crook", learned where the money was held. Since he had a high position in the Armenian Church, he solicited the help of the priest and an influential government friend to "get the money of my dead father." Using threats and bribes, and any other illegal means imaginable, he succeeded in getting the bank to release all of the parents' money to him. Then he taunted the helpless hostage that he had made her penniless, and that he'd let her starve to death. The daughter-in-law now forced Hosanna to work long hours doing all the menial tasks of servants.

Hosanna bided her time patiently, slaving away all day, and watching for a chance to escape. One day her step daughter-in-law left her unguarded, and she fled on foot to Ashods. She wept uncontrollably as Diamondola drew the malnourished, terrorized woman into her home. "They'll soon have me dead. I can't stand any more suffering. If you cannot keep me, I'll sleep on your doorstep," she sobbed. Hosanna slipped off her dress to show Diamondola her many bruises.

"Of course, we'll keep you. We won't let them hurt you anymore," Diamondola promised.

"But I'm afraid. They made me their slave, and they'll be after me." And the poor woman, trembling with fear, burst into tears again.

She was right. In a few days the enraged daughter-in-law beat on Ashods door. "I demand that you bring out that wretched woman and let me take her home where she belongs."

Diminutive Diamondola stood her ground against the insolent, husky woman. "I'll not bring her out to you. You have robbed, enslaved, and abused her."

"Lies! LIES!" she screamed. "We'll get her yet. And don't try to come to my house to get any of her things—ANYTHING!" she ranted as she stomped down the steps uttering curses and threats.

The next day the wicked son, with an officer from the Armenian Church and his government friend, stood yelling at Ashods' door. Hosanna hid while Diamondola faced the angry men alone. The commotion attracted quite a group from the mission office. They listened agape to the son rave insanely, "The Ashods tried to rob me of my inheritance. Now they have stolen my beloved step-mother. I will get all the Adventists expelled from Iran or jailed."

Some of the Adventists were intimidated by his threats and called Diamondola aside. "Maybe Hosanna should go with him to assuage his anger. There is no telling what trouble he and his cronies will cause. Don't get the church involved," they begged.

For a short time Diamondola was uncertain as to what she should do. She was caught between pressure from the mission workers, the babbling idiot, and her own conscience. She offered a quick prayer for help, and almost immediately the strong conviction came over her that she must save Hosanna from her persecutors. She faced the men calmly, but firmly, "I'm not afraid of you. I know that in the sight of God, I am doing what is right by providing a refuge for Hosanna. She will no longer be your slave nor take your beatings. You've made her a human wreck."

The young men with young Kedarian seemed shocked at this revelation; they were unaware that Hosanna had been mistreated. They backed away from the door and took off down the steps. But the vindictive son persisted, "I'll force her back. You'll see." Then he tramped down the stairs.

For a week Diamondola, her mother, and Hosanna prayed that no harm would come to the church, the Ashods, or Hosanna. Then one day as they prayed, Diamondola got a strong impression which she promptly obeyed. She called Gulum Riza, the burly mission gardener and handy man, and together they went over to the Kedarians. The daughter-in-law was there alone. When she saw Gulum standing in her doorway flexing his Herculean muscles, she stepped aside and let the two enter. "We are here to get Hosanna's clothing, bedding, and all of her belongings. Please show us where they are," Diamondola demanded. Gulum cast a surprised glance at Diamondola. He could hardly believe that this demure lady could generate so much spunk.

Mistress Kedarian was dumbfounded. She led them to the servant's quarters, pointed out Hosanna's possessions and, without a word of protest, watched while Gulum gathered them up.

"Thank you," Diamondola said as they left. By nightfall, Hosanna was safely sheltered in Ashods' house of refuge—right along with Kristin.

Chapter 15

HELPING THE HELP MEETS

Gradually Hosanna's frazzled nerves began to mend as she integrated with the Ashod household. Her willing hands were more than useful in helping Theodora run the home. Diamondola and Kristin were always busy with mission work, Bible studies, visits to the sick, or making plans for the forth-coming wedding.

Before the wedding could take place, however, the Ashods were moved to Sultanabad where Aram would do double duty. He continued to keep the mission books and, at the same time, managed the business for the Sultanabad Adventist Hospital.

Sultanabad was a small town important for its carpet industry. Some of Joseph's relatives lived there, and immediately they made the Ashods feel welcome. With deliberate pleasure they spread the news of the forth-coming wedding of Joseph to his bride from Istanbul. Soon the whole village was astir, assuming they would all be invited to the wedding. The Ashods were aghast! As the bride's guardians were they expected to prepare a wedding feast for all the town's people?!?!? Since Ashods were new in Sultanabad, they didn't want to alienate anyone; there-fore, they extended an open invitation to the town's folk.

In a remarkable way, God had prepared a home for the Ashods which could adequately accommodate crowds. When they first moved to Sultanabad, Ashods could not rent a house big enough to fill the needs of their enlarged family, so they converted an unused wing of the hospital into an apartment. The rooms were enormous. Spacious archways naturally annexed adjoining rooms. This arrangement was perfect for the wedding reception.

There were no pastry shops in Sultanabad, so Diamondola, Theodora, and Hosanna spent two weeks preparing cakes and cookies for the wedding reception.

When the wedding day arrived, the food was ready, the decorations in place, and the guests on time. The people were impressed with the Adventist wedding ceremony. They polished off the food, then stayed for the celebration. Ashods played festive music on their phonograph while some of the guests performed folk dances; others told stories or played games. Even though the city turned off the electricity at midnight, the guests were not ready to leave yet. Ashods lit lamps and set them about the house and garden. About one in the morning, the guests finally departed, tired but happy. The whole affair had been a magnificent success. Before retiring, the Ashod household took a quick look at the wedding gifts—beautifully crafted pieces of silver, lovely linens, and many practical household items. Though Kristin was an orphan and a foreigner, the gifts proved that she now had a family of town people who had adopted her.

The newly-weds were anxious to move to Kermanshah where the mission had appointed them to do evangelistic work. However, they couldn't leave until their marriage was legally registered. Before the wedding, Aram and Joseph had spoken to the Armenian priest, who was the official responsible for the registration of Christian marriages. He told them that since the two parties were carrying different citizenship papers—Turkish and Iranian—they would have to get permission from his superior. So Aram and Joseph sought the superior official requesting his immediate attention in the matter. He said, "I don't have the official papers now, but go ahead with the wedding and the permission will come."

Now that the wedding was over, Aram and Joseph went back to see the official. They were told to come back the next day. The next day they were invited to come back again in a few days.

After numerous delays it was obvious that the official wanted a bribe. Aram felt that bribery was taking dishonest advantage of a public office. Finally his patience was exhausted. "Come with me," he ordered Joseph and a relative who worked at a bank. "You will translate for me." He said, pointing to the relative.

"B-but you know Farsee well," protested the relative.

"Well, today I don't. Translated English is more impressive, and I intend to be overpoweringly impressive," Aram muttered between clenched teeth.

Aram and company brushed past the guards and swept into the government official's inner office unannounced. At Aram's direction the two men sat down on the sofa facing the officer's desk. "Wh-what do you want?" stammered the officer, probably thinking he was facing an assassin's bullet.

Aram stood and spoke English. The relative translated. "I am the guardian of the orphan girl who is now married to this young man." He gave Joseph such a resounding slap on the back it almost sent him sprawling. "You have delayed issuing their legal marriage registration. I know Iranian law, and there is no justification for this meaningless postponement."

The officer was obviously shaken, but with pretended bravado said, "Well, what can I do? The permission has not come yet from Teheran. Give me money, and I'll send them a telegram."

Aram stood his ground. "No, if you must send a telegram, that is your responsibility, not mine. We will wait here until we get the registration. If it is not granted today, I will write to the Turkish ambassador, and you (pointing at Joseph) will write to His Majesty. Everyone knows that the Iranian Shah encourages any citizen to write to him if he feels he has suffered an injustice from an official. And if this becomes an issue of political importance, you (pointing at the official) will be responsible." Aram straightened himself and his jacket, satisfied that he had delivered quite an effective speech.

At the translation of Aram's message, the officer's face froze. "Pul-lease be seated in the next room for a few moments while I send a telegram."

Aram's blood pressure subsided considerably as he smiled to himself and took his seat in the next room. His two companions followed in silence staring at Aram in disbelief. Aram? Their soft-spoken missionary? Demanding justice so forcefully?

Aram looked at the two perplexed faces still eyeing him. Slightly embarrassed, he chuckled, "Well, sit down and stop gawking at me. I've been in control the whole time. I felt impressed to say what I said. I am the helper helping the help meets, Joseph and Kristin. Sometimes a Christian has to do what he has to do."

Joseph and the relative exhaled deeply and nodded.

Within five minutes the official appeared, "We've just received the telegram granting permission. You may pick up your papers at the priest's place today."

Aram thanked the official, grabbed his two stupefied companions by the arms and left. That afternoon when Joseph and Aram went to pick up the papers, the Armenian priest laughed, "Who does the officer think he's fooling? We all know he didn't have time to get a telegram back from Teheran. He sent a messenger boy to me with orders to complete the registration papers pronto and have them waiting for you. Here they are."

Joseph and Kristin soon left for Kermanshah where they worked successfully.

And everyone lived happily ever after—well, almost.

Chapter 16

SHARING BREAD WITH THE HUNGRY

Now that the Gabriels were married and gone, Ashods expected life to settle down into a comfortable routine. But that was not on God's agenda.

Summer pressed down upon them with days of relentless heat and hot-weather diseases. The ordinary Sultanabad native was acclimated to this weather, but for the Rumanian and Russian refugees it was a nightmare—a condition from which they could not extricate themselves. To escape Communism, they had fled south to Iranian cities. Then the Iranian government decided to re-distribute them among various cities in Iran lest the great influx of people upset the local economy and work force. This was a brilliant idea except for the refugees who were moved into these small towns. In Sultanabad, for instance, there were no jobs for refugees since every family ran their own business or farm; there was no housing available since every family lived in their own house; and there was no food, clothing, or medical care since there were no government welfare programs. The helpless, starving refugees huddled together on Sultanabad's vacant lot, using polluted water and subsisting on food they could find in the meadows. Sometimes kind Iranians gave the refugees food from their meager store.

The few Adventists in Sultanabad were cognizant of the refugees' plight and went out to help them. They found four very undernourished children dying of dysentery. Their condition was so precarious that Diamondola decided to take them home with her and treat them herself. The little Assyrian, Susan, just Indra's age, was in the worst condition. The three Rumanian children, Andre, 13, Feeza, 9, and Marusa, 6, appeared to have a better chance.

Diamondola got out her medical journals. "Give them boiled water with lemon juice in it for the first 24 hours," she read. She did it. "The next day add grated, raw, ripe apple to the diet." She did that. "For the next few days add boiled rice soup with lemon." She did that too, and the patients' health improved. "Gradually add more foods to the diet as the patient tolerates them." She added food, and the patients were soon up and about.

All four children recovered from dysentery, but they were still undernourished. Now Diamondola's goal was to fatten them up. She invited them to spend the days at her home where they could play in the garden under the coolness of the shade trees and eat two good meals a day at her table. The parents, who had once been wealthy people, were very thankful though embarrassed to accept charity. For the sake of their children, however, they agreed to the plan. Andre maintained a degree of pride. He refused to eat until he had done some work to "earn his keep." The hospital had many fruit trees, flower beds, and gardens to care for, consequently, it was not difficult to find something useful for Andre to do. Indra was happy with her refugee playmates. She almost hated to see them go home at night.

Diamondola frequently took her little brood out to the country for picnics. According to an ancient Biblical custom in the Middle East, the wayfarer may pick as much fruit in the orchards as he can eat, but he must not carry away any produce. The hungry refugee children loved this arrangement; they could pick and eat the wonderful Iranian fruit to their heart's content. The caring farmers sometimes filled baskets of fruit for the children to take back to the camp with them.

By the end of the summer, the children were well and strong. They had learned to enjoy Sabbath School and church. That winter the Rumanian family emigrated to another country. The Ashods hoped the children would remember what they had learned during the summer spent in their home. They prayed that, wherever they went, the children would find God's people and worship with them.

Susan continued to spend her days with the Ashods, going home only at night. Diamondola sewed twin dresses for Indra and Susan, who were now inseparable. But time and providence moves on.

In the late summer of 1936 Ashods were surprised by a call from the Greek mission inviting Aram to join their ministerial staff. Ashods' response circled the normal emotional spectrum—joy at the thought of being reunited with members of the Keanides family (Susanna and her family, and Alexandra still lived in Thessolonica), sorrow at leaving their work and friends in Iran, and concern to know the Lord's will.

After prayerful consideration, they accepted the call. But even while disposing of some household items and packing, the premonition of a disappointment kept haunting them.

Chapter 17

THE LONG, LONG JOURNEY BACK

The first few days of October were rather hectic for the Ashods. They were busy purchasing tickets, crating goods, buying medicine (mother Theodora was ill again), and finishing up mission business in Sultanabad. The hardest part, as always, was saying goodbye. Indra and Susan were broken hearted as they separated forever, and the strain of it all was almost more than Diamondola's delicate system could tolerate.

Hosanna was despondent and anxious about the move. "May God reward you for your kindness to me these past two years. I am obliged to you because I have not been able to pay for my keep. Now you are out more expense in buying my ticket to Beirut. When I get there, what if I cannot find my step-son? Or if I do, what if he doesn't want to take care of me? Where will I go?"

"With us to Greece," Diamondola assured her.

"But I don't want to be a burden to you for the rest of my life!" Hosanna protested.

"Hosanna, have we ever made you feel like you were a burden to us?" Diamondola remonstrated. "You have pulled your share of the household tasks, and we have enjoyed your company. Now let me hear no more of this nonsense. I am too tired to debate the subject."

Everything was "ready, set, go" on October 6, 1936. Hosanna, Theodora, Diamondola, Aram, and little Indra left Sultanabad.

They motored to the first big city, Hamadan, where they spent the night and visited the traditional tombs of Esther and Mordecai.

"Whether Mordecai and Esther are really buried here is irrelevant to me," Aram said. "The fact that Persia names them in their history authenticates the Bible for me."

They traveled west to Kermanshah. There they enjoyed a five-day reunion with Joseph and Kristin. From there it was rough terrain and mountainous roads until they reached the Iraqi border. Indra and Diamondola were car sick most of the way, Theodora was still ill, and Hosanna was apprehensive. All the while Aram hovered over the ailing women. He was relieved when he got them on the train at Hanikan bound for Baghdad.

Baghdad, located on a desert plain on the banks of the Tigris River, has a mysterious enchantment about it that has attracted the attention of authors. Stories like *Ali Baba and his Forty Thieves, A Thousand And One Nights*, etc. intrigue readers everywhere. Although the Ashods had read these charming stories in school, they found the real Bagdad even more fascinating than they imagined. Curiosity and pleasure lured them into bazaars and archeological museums. They ate the exotic foods and devoured the luscious dates. (Iraq produces two-thirds of the world's dates, and in October every variety known to agronomists is available—soft, fresh, fat, delectable dates.)

Their stay in Bagdad revived their spirits, even though five of those days were the hottest the Ashods had ever known. One evening when they returned to their hotel, they found the beds had been removed from their rooms. Aram went down to the desk.

"I'm accustomed to having beds in the rooms I rent," he stated tactfully to the desk clerk, though inwardly he was a bit miffed.

"Yes, yes," the clerk agreed, attempting to use his best English since Aram did not know Arabic. "We take bed to roof. We tink you like sleep up dere—cool. Be hot in room."

Ashods went up to the roof to investigate. Sure enough! Not only were their beds on the flat, cement roof, but all of the other hotel guests' beds were there as well.

"So much for privacy!" complained Diamondola. "I've always dreamed of sleeping on a roof full of conglomerate strangers, mostly business men, when it is too hot to cover one's self with a sheet. We women will have to sleep in our clothes!"

"My Dear, you can have privacy. Sleep under your mosquito net," Aram teased.

Diamondola continued fussing until she got back to their room where the oppressive heat almost made her faint. Then she decided that sleeping unisex on the roof was preferable to an all-night sauna. The ladies undressed in the room and wore housecoats to the roof. By that time, it had cooled off enough so that they could pull their sheets over them. "Ah, a thousand and one nights in enchanting Baghdad," Diamondola sighed as she gazed at the myriad of stars studding the deep-blue sky. Then she drifted off into a restful sleep.

Now that the ladies were as far as Baghdad, Aram could return to Iran to finish up some mission business. First he took the four—Indra, Diamondola, Mother Theodora, and Hosanna—down to the depot and put them on a bus that crossed the trackless Syrian Desert. Then he wired ahead for the mission workers in Damascus to meet his family and transfer them to the train for Beirut.

Soon after they left Baghdad, another passenger incited Diamondola's anxiety by telling her how thieves had stopped last night's bus and robbed the passengers, even taking their clothing. Diamondola sucked in her breath. She certainly hoped that the bandits were not planning an encore. Added to that concern was the fear of the driver getting lost or the bus breaking down. She wondered how the driver could pick his way across the monotonous terrain with no apparent signs or landmarks. She concluded that he, like the wisemen of old, followed the stars.

Next she worried if their bodies would tolerate the jostling in the bus as it lurched over boulders, sand hills, and ravines. Whenever a bump launched her light frame into space, she feared she would land on someone else. As they ground through loose sand, she prayed they would not get stuck; at the same time, she dampened handkerchiefs for her family to hold over their noses to filter the dust that drifted up through the floor boards.

Toilet breaks jeopardized their modesty. There were no shrubs or large boulders on the desert floor to hide behind. The bus driver had the best solution, "Ladies on the left side of the bus and men on the right." Oh well, forget modesty! Probably everyone peeked, anyway.

After 24 hours the dusty, cartilage-shattering journey was over, and they rested safely in Damascus. It took only a few days for their vertebrae to get re-aligned, and then the mission workers put them on the train for Beirut. The smooth trip by train through two mountain ranges covered with fruit trees, umbrella pines, and stone houses with red-tile roofs, was a blessed contrast to their bleak desert crossing. They enjoyed every scenic minute of it. In Beirut they were met by mission personnel and escorted to the Armenian Adventist Church. On Sabbath Diamondola was thrilled to meet again with members of the pre-war churches of Turkey—Iconium, Akshehir, Brousa, Ovadjik, and Caesaria. She had last seen them, starved and dehumanized, on the exile trail. She and Elder Frauchiger had tried to help them. Those who survived and escaped to Beirut assured her that she HAD been the encouragement they needed, and that the blankets and food Diamondola and Frauchiger had brought helped them survive that hazardous trek. (See *Diamondola*, chapter 25)

Hosanna was more than happy to discover her younger step-son in church that Sabbath. After the hugging and tears of joy were over, he insisted that Hosanna go right home with him. He promised to take care of her for the rest of her days. This promise he faithfully and lovingly fulfilled. Hosanna's last days were happy ones. They never heard from the wicked son again.

On October 27, 1936, Diamondola, Theodora, and Indra told Hosanna goodbye, and boarded the Greek ship, ALIKA, for Salonika (Thessolonica), Greece. Six days later they were met at the docks by Alexandra, Susanna, her husband and son, Uncle Stephanos and wife, their married sons and daughters and grandchildren, and a host of other relatives. What a homecoming that was! For a month they received visitors, and the next month they returned the visits. Never in their lives had Diamondola and her mother enjoyed such happy times. Perhaps this would last forever since Aram was now to work in Greece.

By March of 1937, Aram had finished his work in Iran and arrived in Greece. He immediately began the procedures to secure their permanent Greek residence permits. They were issued temporary permits which they would need to renew every three months, but they were assured they would be getting permanent residence permits after a year. No need to worry.

Aram was not comfortable with this arrangement. He felt that the government was stalling. He suspected that they were spying on him too. As a precaution, he asked the mission headquarters in Basil, Switzerland to send his checks and all correspondence in plain envelopes with no return address. In July, however, someone in the Basil office carelessly sent Aram a letter with the mission letterhead on it and a return address. The letter had been censored, and the letterhead had been circled in red. Though the $150 pay roll check was still enclosed, Ashods knew they had cause for concern.

In August it was time for Ashods to renew their temporary permits. They applied, were turned down, and were given notice that they must leave the country no later than August 22. Greece did not want Protestant ministers, and now they knew Aram was one. This was the result of that one letter mailed from Switzerland by someone who gave no thought to the consequences. Diamondola was heartsick. Now she had to leave Greece and her loved ones—perhaps forever. Sometimes she was angry with the careless person in the Basil mission office who had put her whole family in jeopardy.

The church members were equally disappointed. Miss Julia suggested, "I have an influential friend in the Internal Security Office. If I give him a sum of, say 5000 drachmas, I'm sure he can bribe other officials to give you a permit."

The Ashods had never given bribes to anyone before, but they were persuaded that it was worth a try. They gave Miss Julia the sum of money when she left their house that night. In the morning, she was to go to her friend and barter for the permit. That night as Ashods prayed, they felt impressed that if they bought their way into the country, they might stifle some plan God had for them. First thing the next morning Aram went to Miss Julia and asked her to cancel the plan. Fortunately, Miss Julia still had the money. The night before she had gone to her friend's house to implement the scheme, but the friend was not home. Aram took this as a sign from God that he had made the right choice, even though he knew they would have to leave Greece.

The deadline date was fast approaching and concern was mounting. They were people without a country. Where would they go?

At last the mission sent a telegram: GO TO ISTANBUL.

Diamondola's heart sank—not back to Turkey! Not to the land that had been so hostile to them! The very thought made her depressed. She had been so euphorically happy the past nine months; now she must leave her family behind, perhaps never to see them again.

This was the fulfillment, then, of the nagging premonition she had had back in Sultanabad. She dreaded the days ahead.

Chapter 18

TO TURKEY AGAIN

"Aram, please read verses 65 and 66 of Deuteronomy 28. That fits us if we go back to Turkey," Diamondola said dabbing at the tears in her eyes.

Aram opened his Bible and read, "Among those nations you will find no repose, no resting for the sole of your foot. There the Lord will give you an anxious mind, eyes weary with longing, and a despairing heart. You will live in constant suspense, filled with dread both day and night, never sure of your life." He walked over to the couch where Diamondola was sitting and settled himself beside her. "My Darling," he said tenderly, kissing her cheek, "that was what would happen to the WICKED Israelites if they forsook God."

"Well, that's what happens to God's workers in Turkey," Diamondola argued. "We have anxious minds, despairing hearts, constant suspense, and are filled with dread."

"Yes, I remember. I have mixed feelings about going back to Turkey myself," Aram admitted. "I'm anxious to see old friends and continue the mission work, but I dread facing the daily uncertainties there."

Their concerns were justified. Almost as soon as the boat docked at Istanbul the customs officials came aboard and called the Ashods aside. Usually customs officials inspect the passenger's goods, but these men confiscated all of Ashods' written materials—sermons, memos, correspondence, journals, every-thing typed or written by hand.

Instinctively they knew this meant trouble. Diamondola remembered some papers in their files that would be particularly incriminating for her. It was the twelve stories she had written in 1920 about the orphan children who had escaped the genocide, persecutions, and atrocities that the Turks had inflicted on the Christians at that time. Those articles alone could land her in jail. But what she feared most was their finding the copy of the cover letter she had sent with the stories. That letter had the mission address and her personal signature which positively identified her as the author. With that letter as evidence, they could arrest her as a traitor. Then what? The gallows, imprisonment, exile? She knew it was paramount that they retrieve the letter. She was so frightened she began to cry.

"Please," she begged, "give me back all of my personal corre-spondence. Among them are my recipes which I have spent years collecting from friends all over the world."

But the officers remained indifferent to her plea. "When we are finished, Madame, we will send for you."

"I'm sure of that," Diamondola thought grimly. "I'd probably ought to try to escape Turkey now." But then she reconsidered. "My God is a great God, and He has always delivered me. Besides, if God sent us back to Turkey to work He won't desert us now."

Those thoughts reassured her for the moment, but during the next few days Diamondola found herself vacillating between trust and fear. The suspense of waiting gnawed away at the core of her faith.

After a week Aram was called to the customs house. "To whom do these papers belong?" he was asked by an irate customs official pointing to the pack of stories.

"To whomever the original copies were sent," he answered, sweat pouring from his brow. "It is some one in America whose name I do not recall." (He honestly didn't know to whom Diamondola had mailed them.)

They seemed satisfied with his answer, and, fortunately, did not ask him who had sent or written the stories. If they had, it would have been extremely difficult for Aram to have divulged the name of the author.

After three more weeks of agonizing suspense, they were called again to the customs house. With trepidation, they made their way there, not knowing what to expect but certain the matter was in God's hands.

The customs officers gave them back a mess of papers stuffed in a bag. When the Ashods got home, they sifted through the papers and were not surprised to see the stories were missing. The damaging letter with Diamondola's signature was not there, either. What could this mean? Were they preparing a case against her?

Diamondola was distraught. She picked up her recipe box and sat nervously fingering through the cards. Suddenly she came across a folded paper. Strange! She only kept cards in the box. Curious, she pulled it out. To her astonishment she was holding THE LETTER—the one piece of evidence that could link her to the stories. Since she had written all the stories, she had never bothered to sign them. She had only signed the cover letter. Now she was in possession of the evidence. She relaxed for the first time that month.

"How do you suppose that letter got in there, Aram?"

"I don't have positive proof, Diamondola, but I suspect your angel folds letters and puts them in recipe boxes."

Chapter 19

SECRET MEETINGS

During the month the Ashods waited for their papers to be returned, they exercised their faith. Believing that they would be permitted to stay in Turkey, they hunted for a house to rent. After Ashods left Turkey in 1931, the first and third floors of the mission-owned apartment building had been rented to non-Adventists. There were no workers in Istanbul needing the apartments at that time, and the rental money came in handy to cover operating expenses. Elder Klinger, mission president, and his family occupied the second floor of the mission house. Now that Ashods were back, they tried to get one of the mission apartments. They could not do so, however, because Turkish law stated that a renter could not be evicted as long as he paid his rent. The mission leaders knew the renters would not move, even though this posed a hardship on Ashods.

The Ashods were relieved when the matter of the papers was resolved, and a resident permit was granted to them. They found a suitable house in the suburbs of Kadikoy and resigned themselves to work in Turkey. Now that the family was settled, Aram searched for a suitable meeting place for the church congregation. This was not easy.

Turkish law limited all church services or meetings to an officially recognized church building. The Adventists did not own a church anywhere in Turkey at this time. Since the law was strictly enforced, it was paramount that they find rental space in another Christian church. The trouble was that the other Christian churches did not want to rent their buildings to the Adventists.

The General Conference was aware of this problem in Turkey, but at this point in time, they couldn't do anything about it. Everyone knows that hind sight has 20/20 vision. Critics felt that there was a time when the General Conference could have built a church but was too slow in acting. There were several factors that influenced their decision. The Adventist message entered Turkey in 1889 with the return of Theodore Anthony, a shoemaker, who had been converted in California. During that first decade, the fledgling group was too few in number to warrant the expenditure of building a church. In the early 1900's, the mission probably could have secured permission to build a church. But during that period, the missionaries, due to illnesses, came and left like whistle stops—no one stayed long enough to put down roots and initiate the project. If two mission families had been stationed in Turkey at the same time, there might have been enough continuity in the work to have applied for and received legal recognition for the Adventist church. As it was, the Adventists were not recognized as a legal church by the Turkish government before World War I. Without that legality, anything they would have built could have been confiscated; in fact, that was the case in the other towns where Adventist members had built churches.

After the war, it was too late. The Luzanne Treaty specified that no Christian churches could be built in Turkey. Aram tried to get the Turkish officials to circumvent this law a little when the mission purchased the apartment property in 1926. He suggested that they could remove basement partitions in the mission house, make a separate entrance for the members, and meet there unobtrusively. The petition was kindly but firmly rejected. The government feared that one exception would set a precedence, and the country would soon be blossoming with Christian churches.

When Ashods left for Iran in 1931, the 75 members, plus visitors, met on Sabbath mornings in the dark, crowded basement of a Protestant church. It was lighted with kerosene lamps, heated with an old wood-burning stove, and furnished with rough, backless wooden benches. It was not ideal, but it was legal. How the members wished they would be permitted to use the church proper! The upstairs sanctuary was furnished with electric chandeliers, Turkish carpets, and pews—all of which lent comfort and beauty to the worship service. The Protestants stiffly refused the Adventists' overture to rent the sanctuary, even though their own small membership of only fifteen people urgently needed the extra money. The committee further stipulated that the Adventists were not to proselytize their members, publicize their meetings, or leave or hand out any literature.

The Adventists cooperated with their demands. In spite of the restrictions put upon them, the Adventist membership continued to grow rapidly. This incited a degree of jealousy on the part of the host church. About this time, the government, in a move to create better relations with the Christians, called an advisory-type meeting to which each church could send one delegate. One of the Adventist brethren very foolishly appointed himself as the Adventist representative and went to the meetings. He didn't realize that by doing so, he would be displacing the Protestant representative. This presumptuous action justifiably angered the host church, and they kicked the Adventists out of their basement.

The Adventists were then forced to meet secretly in homes. One Sabbath the police broke into one of the home meetings and took all the worshipers off to jail. After two hours the police chief came to investigate the law breakers. He examined them one by one. It was Asnive, the sister-in-law of Baharian (the first ordained national preacher in Turkey) whom God used to save them. She told the officer, "We don't just study the Bible, we pray to Allah too." She felt impressed to say this because she knew that the sincere Moslem prays five times daily, kneeling toward Mecca with his forehead touching the ground or floor.

"You do? What prayers do you repeat?" the officer asked, obviously interested.

"No memorized prayer," Asnive explained. "We just pray for what is on our hearts." And then, before the officer had a chance to question her further, she dropped to her knees, offered a simple prayer, and concluded by asking God to bless the officer and his family. He was so startled and touched that he dismissed the entire group.

This experience did not end or solve their future problems, however. Since the Adventists had a compelling desire to meet together for worship, they knew someone, sooner or later, would report them.

"Well, we're back to square one," Aram sighed somewhat discouraged. "I've spent the day contacting every Christian church in town, and all of them have refused to rent to us. We'll have to continue to meet in small groups in houses. This means I will preach to two of the four companies each Sabbath, while Brother Kalustyan will speak to the other two groups. Do you suppose, Diamondola, that you can pull an "Asnive" maneuver, just in case we need it?"

"If we get arrested, I'll do whatever the Lord impresses me to do."

One of the places the members met was in Ashods' house in Kadikoy. Knowing the gamble they took in meeting illegally, the Ashods kept their home clear of written materials that might cause suspicion. The group formed their chairs in a circle, and Aram used only his Bible; that way it appeared more like a study group than a church service. If they sang at all, they did so very quietly. As a further precaution, Diamondola always kept refreshments handy which would indicate a social affair.

One Sabbath they were startled by a police officer pounding on their door demanding entrance. A Moslem neighbor, probably hoping to gain favor with the authorities, had reported that there were suspicious "political" meetings at Ashods' house every Saturday afternoon. He also claimed that Aram had a hidden transmitter and was involved in spy operations. The neighbor had concocted this perfectly ridiculous story from his fertile imagination. All he really knew was that people went to Ashods' home at a certain time on Saturdays. He could have joined them and learned first hand that the Adventists were the most harmless, non-political, peace-loving citizens in all of Turkey.

The officer searched the house for the transmitter, while the members sat transfixed in their chairs. When he was satisfied that there was no transmitter, and probably never had been, he left. But soon two other officers came. They searched everywhere imaginable—cupboards, drawers, closets, trunks, lights etc. They studied carefully all books, printed materials, and correspondence. This investigation took quite some time. Aram grasped this opportunity to tactfully inform these men about Adventists.

"Gentlemen, I am sure you will find nothing against the government of Turkey in an Adventist's home. We are non-political people who only want peace."

"The Christians of Armenia rose against us during the Great War," they retorted.

"That may have been true of some Christians but never of Adventists. Should we be suspected of subversive activities because of what other Christians have done in the past? That isn't fair," Aram reasoned. "Look around this house. Do you see any icons or images? Doesn't that tell you we are different? We, like the Moslems, pray directly to God. We do not eat pork, drink alcohol, or smoke. In most countries the Moslems feel a kinship to Adventists."

"You would make good Moslems," one officer commented as he looked about. "But do you put the Prophet Jesus above the Prophet Mohammed?"

"Jesus is God, and He is our Savior. Mohammed was a man—though a good man—and your prophet," Aram said. Then he explained the fall of man and God's wonderful plan of redemption though the sacrifice of Jesus Christ. He elaborated on the trinity and other subjects perplexing to Moslems. In one afternoon he gave the officers the whole Bible message in capsulated form. The members learned from the veteran, Aram, while the Moslem officers listened intently to the sweetest story ever told. The officers were touched by the love God had for them.

Many hours later the officers left. Aram praised God that he was able to witness for Him, and the members praised God that no one had been arrested.

Aram appealed once more to the government headquarters in Ankara to allow them to build a small chapel in the mission garden or to arrange one in the basement of the mission house. Again his request was rejected, and the Adventists were obliged to continue to meet secretly.

Small cottage meetings during the week were the safest; the informal service helped many inquirers find answers to their questions. One day while Aram was conducting a cottage meeting, a young lady entered the room. "That's the man!" she exclaimed. "That's the man I saw in my dream!"

Aram was disconcerted by this interruption from someone he'd never seen before. He asked her to tell her dream since everyone wanted to hear about it.

"A few months ago I dreamed that I was at a small gathering where a man was preaching wonderful things from the Bible he held in his hands. You are the man I saw," she said pointing to Aram. "Previous to my dream I had been wondering why we worship before icons, light candles, and perform other rites that seem superfluous to God-worship, but I could find no answers from my Gregorian priests. Then my friend invited me to come here. Now I recognize this is the fulfillment of my dreams. I know God led me here."

God had, and Berjouhie was an avid learner. Soon she was baptized.

Other new members included Timotheus, who worked on the docks, his wife, who worked as a janitor, and their small daughter. They were very poor since neither of them had steady work. One Friday afternoon Diamondola, who was the church treasurer, noticed that the family had not paid tithe for some time. She felt impressed to call on them to discuss tithing. Before she finished talking, Timotheus and his wife were strongly convicted that tithing was right and that they should follow God's instruction. He opened his billfold and drew out all his money—50 piasters, enough to buy basic food for one day. He gave the money to Diamondola saying, "Here, take this. I was going to buy some food for the weekend, but I prefer to honor God with my tithe first."

Diamondola hesitated, and Timotheus detected her dilemma. He pressed the money into her hand saying, "Please take this. It is the Lord's. I want to be honest with Him. I need His spiritual blessings more than I need the food." Then as an after thought, he added, "Like Malachi says, maybe He will open the windows of heaven for us."

When the Lord commands and the Holy Spirit impresses, what can one do?

Diamondola took the money, prayed with them, and left. She was so concerned about Timotheus' family going hungry that she could not eat her own supper. Timotheus' last bit of money was in the tithe envelope on her table staring her in the face. That night, Diamondola and her mother fasted and prayed for this faithful family.

Sabbath morning an excited Timotheus stood up in church. "May I testify?" he asked. Permission was granted and the members listened spellbound. "Yesterday Diamondola called to remind us to be honest and return God's tithe money to Him. For some time our income had been so little that we felt we needed everything we earned to buy food. Well, last evening I gave Sister Diamondola my last money for the tithe I had withheld. She was scarcely gone before God opened His windows on me.

First, the baker next door arrived with two large loaves of his best bread. He said he felt impressed to give them to me. It is a miracle that he should have any left since you know that bread is rationed. A little later our teenage son, who has never contributed anything toward the food bill but spends his money on questionable amusements, came into the house with a basketful of food. There were vegetables, fruit, cheese, and foods we had not eaten for a long time. We could hardly believe our eyes. We have not eaten so sumptuously for months. It's a miracle. My soul is refreshed." Everyone else's soul was also refreshed by his testimony.

The years passed, and the membership continued to grow in spite of the inconvenience and danger involved in meeting illegally. But Aram was not satisfied. "I want all the members to meet together every Sabbath—not in four separate groups. Together we will encourage and strengthen one another. Quite a bit of time has passed since the Protestants barred the Adventists from their church. Now I feel I should appeal to them for re-instatement."

"What gives you hope that they will reconsider?" Diamondola asked.

"I have three reasons: 1) the Protestant membership has grown very little, and they need the money; 2) time erases misunderstandings; and 3) Mikran Govreckian, a relative of your sister's husband, Nazareth, has recently been elected to serve on the Protestant church board. He might use his influence to get the Adventists re-instated."

Aram's hunch paid off. Once more the Adventists were given permission to meet in the basement of the Armenian Protestant church. They longed to meet upstairs but were thankful for small favors. At least for now, they could all be together for Sabbath services, LEGALLY. In the meantime, they would pray that God would "open the Red Sea" for them so they could build a church of their own.

Chapter 20

THE BEST OF TIMES

The Adventist members were very thankful that all of them could meet together for Sabbath School and church services. This freed Ashods' Sabbath afternoons for other activities. They knew that keeping the Sabbath holy could sometimes cause boredom for the restless youth; therefore, they invited them to their home for Bible games, youth meetings, and/or discussions. About sundown they had worship followed by refreshments and party games.

From May through October, Ashods organized Sunday picnics for the whole church by the sea or in the country. They sometimes took the ferry for a day's cruise on the Marmara Sea or up the Bosporus Straits. Some non-Adventist youth asked to join the Christian recreation and Bible meetings. Of course, they were invited to share in both.

Among the non-Adventist members who came to the meetings were Kevork Yeshil, his brother and sister, and Selma and Ayhan Karhraman. Kevork enjoyed the activities but was especially interested in spiritual things. He delighted in studying the Bible with Aram, who patiently explained difficult passages to his satisfaction. Kevork's early years had been spent in Iconium with his parents and siblings. They fled to Istanbul during the 1920's when more persecution of Christians loomed on the horizon. His parents enrolled him in the French Catholic Assumption School. He never understood nor profited much from the rituals in the Gregorian church, but neither did he get much out of the Latin masses at the Catholic Church. He did understand and appreciate their loving care. When his father's business failed, the Catholics allowed the Yeshil children to continue their education even though they could not pay the bill. Kevork, however, had to drop out of school to help support the family. At age 14 he began work as a "go-for" office boy. Two years later his fortune improved when he got work at Orozdi-Bach, a French department store. Thanks to the Catholic Sisters, his French was excellent and so was his desire to please. When he was 19, they made him the youngest-ever department manager in their store. He doubled the sales of his predecessor the first year. The extra pay was badly needed to support his mother, younger sister and brother, and an older sickly brother. His father had died, and the three older children had gone to Europe. It was at this stage in his life that Kevork came in contact with the Adventists. He liked their straight Bible message and the youth fellowship. He also liked Selma, but he dared not express his affection for her. He was in no position financially to consider a serious relationship, but he dreamed he would marry her one day.*

Grief took the place of contentment for the Yeshil family when word reached them that the 26-year old sister in France had died. The mother could hardly cope with the tragedy since she could neither see her daughter's body nor attend the funeral. Two months later the sickly brother died. Mrs. Yeshil's grief was now inconsolable. The Ashods recognized serious suicidal symptoms developing in Mrs. Yeshil. They visited her often and did all they could to help the children cope with the family deaths and their mother's severe depression.

It was at this time that the Ashods rented a new home in Uskudar. The setting was idyllic; the back lawn melted into a country, wooded area. It was a perfect location for youth activities and for Grandma and Indra too.

The Ashods themselves did not have as much time as they wanted to enjoy this paradise, but it proved to be a blessing to others. The first person to need its therapeutic solace was Kevork's mother. One day the doctors told Ashods that Mrs. Yeshil would either die of stress or kill herself. Ashods knew that Kevork did not have the money to put her in a sanitarium so they brought her to their home. They took her for long walks in the woods or by the sea. They read comforting passages from the Bible and prayed with her. They made sure she rested and ate good food. Gradually, life took on new meaning for Mrs. Yeshil. It was a happy day when Ashods could restore her to her family, cured by nature and God.

The days spent at the house in Uskudar filled Ashods' memory bank with pleasant thoughts of the Christian fun they had with the young and the "young at heart" there. Those were the best of times.

*Kevork and Selma eventually married and lived happily with their children in Istanbul.

Chapter 21

SMOKE AND FIRE

World War II shattered the brief period of tranquility and pleasure that the Ashods had enjoyed in Turkey. Hitler's Nazi troops invaded Poland in 1939. This forewarned Ashods of the gathering storm, but they hoped that somehow Turkey could avoid involvement. During the next two years, the smoke of war settled all around them as one country after another capitulated to the Nazi war machine. Turkey was bordered on the north by the Black Sea and Russia, on the west by Bulgaria and Greece, on the east by Iran, and on the south by the Mediterranean Sea, Iraq, and Syria.

After the bombing of Pearl Harbor in December of 1941, the United States declared war on both Japan and Germany. This threw most of the countries in the northern hemisphere into battle array on either one side or the other. Eventually, the Eastern Mediterranean countries—Syria, Lebanon, Palestine, Iraq, Jordan, and Egypt—aligned themselves with the allies. Turkey hoped to remain neutral, but it became increasingly difficult as the conflict closed in around her. Greece fell to the Nazis; Rommel's forces moved across North Africa; Germany and Italy filled the Mediterranean Sea with mines. Turkey began drafting men into the army, just in case they were forced to take sides. Twenty-one year old Kevork was the first to go from the Adventist group.

The news from Greece was not good. The Nazis had taken control of the country's resources, food, and medical supplies, leaving the people to suffer. Now the Ashods were very thankful that they had been forced to leave Greece. They believed God had a hand in their deportation. They were also thankful that Alexandra, who retired from nursing in 1939, had come to Turkey to live with them. Stavro, Susanna's husband had died of a stroke in 1938, but Susanna and her son Pano still lived in Greece. She wrote to Ashods describing their deplorable condition—no food, no fuel, no medicines. Aram mailed many CARE packages to Susanna endeavoring to help them through the days of deprivation. Some got through; others were stolen.

Ashods had no evening meetings during the war. The city was blacked out at night; dark shades were drawn over all windows so not a glimmer of light could be seen from the street. Aram improved the evening hours by helping Indra with her lessons. He was an interesting teacher, and she was a willing student. One particular night, before they began their studies, Aram had a strange foreboding that some calamity was about to befall them. He knelt and prayed. He began the lessons with Indra, but twice more he felt uneasy, and twice more he prayed that God would protect them from whatever impending doom was about to descend. Apprehensively, he looked out upon the peaceful scene—the stars shining down upon the myriad of wooden houses nestled close beside one another. He noticed the dry wind of late summer blowing strongly from the west and thought, "A perfect night for an inferno. One enemy bomb could start a fire that would annihilate our whole quarter in minutes." He let down the black shade, returned to Indra, and tried to crowd out his fears.

Diamondola was tired that night and decided to go to bed early. Leaving Aram and Indra to study, she crossed the hall into the front bedroom, pulled the blind, and crawled into bed. She had just fallen into a deep sleep when she was abruptly awakened by blood-curdling screams. "Mr. Ashod! Come and help us!! OUR HOUSE IS ON FIRE!!!"

Diamondola shot out of bed, landing on both feet in the middle of the floor. In the complete blackness she fumbled for the door, grabbed a knob, turned it, and rushed headlong into the walk-in closet, ramming her head on clothes hangers. She extricated herself from the clothing and tried again. Feeling her way along the wall she burst through the hall door and delivered her message, full volume, 100 decibels, "ARAM! Run and help the neighbor, QUICK! HER HOUSE IS ON FIRE!"

Aram's ear drums were still vibrating from Diamondola's alarm when he rushed out of the house almost modestly clothed. The neighbor man and his wife were frantic. Both they and Aram knew it was impossible for the fire trucks to get there in time to save anything in their house. A strong wind was fanning the flames rapidly throughout the building. She begged Aram to go upstairs and drag down her huge chest full of valuables. Aram flew up the stairs. He tugged and pulled, but the chest was a job for Atlas, not Aram. Then, from the upstairs window, he noticed that fagots from the burning house were sailing through the air unto the roofs of other wooden houses around them. He looked down at his own house—it was on fire!

Aram dashed back across the street yelling to Diamondola, "Collect our valuables and flee from the house! Its going up in flames!" Just as he entered the front door, an explosion punctuated his statement. The searing heat from the neighbor's house had burst the Ashods' front windows. Aram called his household together; hurriedly they knelt and prayed that God would save them, their goods, and the rest of the people in their community.

Then Aram moved with alacrity. He emptied a large suitcase of woolens onto the floor, replaced it with valuables, and sent young Indra and Grandmother lugging it up the hillside in the opposite direction from which the wind was blowing. Next he, Diamondola, and Alexandra carried immense armloads of stuff up the hill, deposited it into the custody of Grandmother, and left for a second load. Adrenalin pumped through their veins giving them Herculean strength to carry furniture and chests. On the third trip back, they found they had locked the front door by accident. Now they couldn't get into the house. They raced around to the back where there was a small, secret door. They tried it, but it was barred from the inside. Though an experienced thief could not have done it, Aram was able to break apart the bars and enter the house. They exited the third time through the back passage and once more climbed the hill with necessary possessions. They made many trips, dragging things through the little back passage. The fire in their house had gone out, but they expected it to start up again. When at last they were satisfied that they had removed the most practical items from the house, they collapsed on the hillside with Indra and Grandmother. A neighbor, whose house was out of the line of the fire, invited them to spend the night with her. The ladies accepted the kind invitation while Aram stayed with their stuff.

The next morning they returned to the scene of destruction. They were amazed to see the damage—over 20 homes were completely destroyed. Many houses were still smoldering because the people had already laid in their winter's supply of wood and coal. Broken glass filled the streets.

Ashods went to the site of their house. What they saw was phenomenal. Their house was standing almost unscathed in the midst of a sea of ashes. While all of the houses around them were burned to the ground, only one corner of their house was even scorched, although the front windows were shattered from the heat. A thief had broken into the secret passage but had not taken much because it was too difficult for him to maneuver anything through the narrow space. Now Ashods could see it was a blessing that their front door had slammed shut and locked. Looters had come and cleaned out the other homes while they were still burning. Most of the people had saved nothing.

Ashods hired a glass cutter to come and put in their front windows. They spent the whole day moving things back into the house. The night before they had carried their belongings UP the hill in just two hours. Items that one of them carried up the hill alone took two and three people to carry back DOWN the hill. They were relieved to get settled again by nightfall but were sorry that their neighbors had suffered such losses. Aram's premonition had been verified, and his prayers for protection were answered.

People wondered why the Ashods' house had been spared so miraculously. Then they remembered. It had been built by a true "Sabbatarian". The owner, who was now dead, had been a very sincere, though poverty-stricken, Seventh-day Adventist. He saved for years to construct this property. He had to hire non-Adventist carpenters to do the building. They insisted upon six days pay but would not work on Sundays. Consequently, the Adventist brother had to pay the carpenters for Sabbaths hours even though they did not work on the house that day. The Ashods rented the house from the man's wife and daughter who lived out of town. The neighbors almost superstitiously believed that the house was miraculously spared by God in honor of his devout steward. Could they have been right?

Chapter 22

MOVING ON TO BETTER THINGS

The war still raged throughout the world in 1943, and its outcome was uncertain. Osters left Turkey, and Aram became the mission president. The Ashods moved into the mission apartment and on to better things—they hoped.

Back of them lived the Gomik family. This arrangement was especially nice since the two families had been friends for many years. During the genocide of the Christians following World War I, Mr. and Mrs. Gomik and their three children were captured and sent on the exile trail. When Elder Frauchiger and Diamondola made their relief mission into the interior of Turkey to help the deportees, they found the Gomiks huddled in a shack in a village of the Iconium district. Though they were destitute and starving, they somehow survived and eventually made their way to Istanbul. The Gomiks soon endeared themselves to the members in Istanbul as they participated actively in the church work.

The youngest Gomik child was Ebraxie. She was a very intelligent girl, and the Gomiks sacrificed everything to give her the best education possible. After she completed high school, they sent her to the Armenian Yessayan School, a junior college in the city. Sometimes she was urged to attend classes or other activities on the Sabbath, but Ebraxie stood firm, and the administration honored her convictions.

The real crisis came during her last year in the college. The government had appointed a Turkish associate principal who insisted that some of the senior classes which met on Sabbath were too important for Ebraxie to miss, but Ebraxie refused to attend them. Her Armenian principal/head teacher, who had been cooperative with her convictions in the past, now urged Ebraxie to change her mind. "It's your last year," she argued. "Just go to school on Saturdays this year, and God will excuse you. Then you can keep holy all the rest of the Sabbaths of your life. You are too close to finishing your education to give it up now. Ebraxie, please cooperate."

But Ebraxie could not be tempted. "My faithfulness in the past does not give me dispensation to break the commandment now."

"Then," advised the principal, "you must leave the school since you cannot graduate without attending these classes."

Ashods were concerned for Ebraxie and prayed that God would help her stand firm by her decision. They knew it was not easy for her. Often they would look down from their balcony and see Ebraxie walking in the garden crying. She was so close to graduation; it was truly a pity that she could not complete her education.

The Ashods and other close friends set aside a special day of fasting and prayer for Ebraxie. If the Turkish director would not change her mind and allow Ebraxie to complete her last year of school, they prayed that Ebraxie would have the courage to remain faithful. The Adventists in Turkey had learned to live by faith. Consequently, they were not surprised when ten days later Ebraxie was called back to the school. She graduated that spring. Ebraxie had honored God, and He honored her. Following graduation she went to Beirut, Lebanon, where, she taught in the Armenian Adventist School.

Two years later World War II ended, rationing ended, and the Adventists in Turkey hoped to see a big influx of converts. For this purpose, they brought Ebraxie back to Istanbul as a Bible worker. With fresh zeal the church pushed forward.

It was at this juncture that Diamondola got a letter from Mrs. Agnes Frauchiger inviting her and Indra to come to Switzerland for the summer. Agnes wrote that her husband was no longer with her, and she longed to see a familiar face. Although the two friends had corresponded regularly, it had been 30 years since they had seen each other.

Diamondola could not resist the tempting invitation. In August of 1947, Diamondola and Indra were off for the best vacation of their lives. They boarded a ship for Naples, Italy. From there they hopped a train for Rome, Milan, and Lucerne. They enjoyed the sights in Italy but nothing could compare with the tranquility of the Swiss Alps. They relaxed and walked with Agnes, talking a steady stream in an attempt to fill in the gaps of a 30-year absence. All the while they were enjoying the sights and scents of the pastoral country.

The Erzbergers also lived in Switzerland; the vacation would not be complete without seeing them after a 25-year separation. Erzbergers took them to camp meeting in Basil where they met more former members and missionaries from Turkey. What a thrill this vacation proved to be!

Former workers and members, who had escaped the Kemalist movement, called Diamondola to visit them in France. The next thing they knew, Diamondola and Indra were exploring exciting Paris and Marseille. Old friends showed them tourist attractions until they felt certain they could absorb no more.

All too soon the summer vacation ended. Diamondola and Indra returned to Istanbul completely rejuvenated. "The only thing better than a European vacation," Indra told her father, "is heaven. There I will be self-propelled and can visit our friends every day. It will be even prettier than the Alps."

The winter following the grand vacation, Indra finished middle school in Istanbul and was ready for high school. Ashods disliked parting with their only child, but they knew it was best to send Indra to Middle East College Preparatory School in Beirut. One consoling factor was that Shahin Ilter, Indra's cousin, worked at the college. Shakee, one of Ebraxie's converts, was also going to MEC. The parents believed that giving the girls a Christian education was the best way to insure a spiritual foundation for them.

After Shakee and Indra left, the mission gave the Ashods two calls to go to other places to work. They could go to Dar-es-Salaam hospital in Baghdad, or they could go to Cyprus. As they prayed about their choices, they felt they could do the most good in Cyprus. People on that island spoke Turkish, Greek, Armenian, and English. Ashods knew all four languages. In Iraq, the main language was Arabic which they did not know. Their third choice was to stay in Turkey where they had just completed a ten-year stint. They reasoned that it might be better for them and the work to have a change.

Leaving Turkey proved to be a complicated process for Ashods. First, they had to go through many formalities with reams of lists and signatures. There were passports and exit visas to secure. "Who'd have ever thought the Turkish government had such an affinity for us," was Aram's tongue-in-cheek comment. "They weren't thrilled with our return ten years ago. Now their regulations are so complicated it is almost impossible to leave."

The next hurdle was caring for their household goods. According to Turkish law, carpets and silver could not be exported. Now Ashods had to sell their Persian carpets and silver from Iran at a fraction of their value. The irony of it all wrung Diamondola's heart. "It isn't fair, Aram. In our 27 years of married life we have given our all—time, money, talent—to be ambassadors for God in the Middle East. We've spent most of our time and money on the work or people who needed our help. Those carpets we purchased in Iran were an investment; the silver was given to us by friends and is hand-engraved in our names. I'm having to give up family heirlooms and mementos!"

"I know, my Dear. It isn't the carpets, per se; it is the memory of the friends who walked on them. To paraphrase Job, 'naked I came into this world, and the government will make sure we depart from Turkey in the same condition.' We might be going on to better things, but we'll do so a whole lot poorer."

"Well, to paraphrase Peter, 'Silver and carpets have I none', but I do have the gospel message which I can share with the people in Cyprus," Diamondola commented.

On December 10, 1948, Diamondola, Aram, Alexandra, and Mother Keanides sailed from Istanbul on the Turkish steamer, S.S. Kadesh. Even though it was wintertime, the blue Mediterranean Sea was calm and pleasant. They spent most of their nine days on deck enjoying the sunshine and the relaxing effect of the waves lapping gently on the bow of the ship. They stopped at Izmer (old Smyrna, Turkey), Pireus (Greece), Alexandria (Egypt) and Beirut (Lebanon). In Beirut Indra, Shakee, Shahin, Edith, and other friends met them on the dock to visit with them briefly.

Then it was on to Cyprus. Diamondola and Aram stood by the ship's railing as the outline of the island came into view.

"Diamondola," he said, taking her hand, "this is on to better things for God's work and us."

Without hesitation she answered, "I am sure of it. Anywhere the Lord leads is the best place on earth for us. Cyprus will be the fourth country in the Middle East where we have served as God's ambassadors. Aren't we fortunate?"

Chapter 23

THE LAND OF THE FREE, AND SOME WHO WERE BRAVE

As Diamondola stepped off the gangplank onto Cypriot soil, she turned to Aram, her mother, and her sister Alexandra. "Do you see these feet?" she asked. "They are standing on a land that has religious freedom. Here I'll have the liberty to practice my spiritual ambassadorial profession. Think of that! After working 30 years for God, at last my feet are free to carry the gospel to anyone on this island of Cyprus."

The others were slightly amused by Diamondola's dramatic performance, but they were also relieved to be in Cyprus. Here they would not be hampered by government mandates or fear of arrest.

The Ashod family settled in Nicosia, the capital, located approximately in the center of the island. Almost all of the Adventists were concentrated there. They learned that four-fifths of the population in Cyprus were Greek Orthodox Christians and most of the rest were Turkish Moslems.

Since the demise of the Apostolic Sabbath-keeping church, the first Seventh-day Adventist to go to Cyprus was Moses Boursalian. He fled there from Antioch, Turkey, in 1912. He quietly plied his comb-making trade and shared his faith with his neighbors. His son became the first colporteur in Cyprus. After 20 years of concerted effort on the part of the Boursalians, there were only 10 names registered in the church books.

In 1932, Elder and Mrs. R. S. Greaves decided to retire in Cyprus rather than their homeland (Canada) and make this their mission field. They settled in Kirinia, a seacoast town, but their evangelism fell on deaf ears.

"Something serious is wrong here," Diamondola observed. "From 1912 to 1948 is 36 years; yet, there are only 20 Adventists in Cyprus, not counting the workers. Furthermore, most of the Adventists consist of refugees and their children from Turkey. Here we have freedom to preach and distribute literature, but to what avail? Protestantism doesn't seem to be breaking through Cypriot complacence."

"That's right, but we're going to try," Aram said determinedly. "It's good to have Brother Barlas here with his colporteur ministry to help us."

A. N. Barlas would indeed be a help.* He was the fearless soul who had colporteured in Turkey from 1927 through 1946. Barlas didn't even remember how many times he'd been arrested or imprisoned while canvassing in Turkey. He did remember the time at Trabzon, a city on the Black Sea, when an irate police officer arrested him and offered to put a 3-cent bullet through his head. Barlas wasn't fond of that idea. Evidently God wasn't either, for when the officer's anger subsided, he dismissed Barlas without depositing the proffered bullet in his head. Finally, Barlas and his family moved to Cyprus where he hoped his ministry could be more effective and less stressful. He was quite successful in selling his literature in Cyprus, but converts were few.

Ashods and Barlases now planned to unite their evangelistic efforts to try to engender a change. When Aram was not preaching or giving Bible studies, he was busy translating Bible Correspondence lessons into Armenian and Turkish, an additional task the Middle East Division had assigned him.

The Adventists met at the Leontides home for Sabbath Services, but the workers envisioned an increase in membership to the point where they would need to build a regular church. Evangelism, they supposed, was the key to reaching this goal.

Aram found this more difficult than he had imagined. The hall they were finally able to rent was exposed to all the street noise, making it almost impossible to hear. The hammers on the old piano stuck, spoiling every hymn with dissonance. One could almost see through the cracks in the wall. When the people upstairs were active, little crumbs of plaster spilled down from the ceiling. The safest spot in the room was against the inner wall. The rickety chairs and benches wobbled and sometimes collapsed.

"Aram, this room we rented is not a good place for worship," Diamondola declared. "But we are free! No fear of being arrested! After 10 years of constant apprehension, this is a blessed relief. However, this place lacks EVERYTHING. The Cypriot, Sergius Paulus, of the Apostle Paul's day would never come here. This furniture is so rickety and unrepresentative, I doubt that even the trash collectors would accept it."

"I know," Aram concurred. "Hardly anyone attends the meetings either. But to make sure we get our money's worth out of it, we'll hold Sabbath services here until the rent runs out. This will give the Leontides home a brief respite."

Transportation was another problem for the Ashods. They were accustomed to the fine public transportation facilities in Turkey. There was no such luxury on the island. There were very few private cars and only a few taxis and buses. Almost everyone in Cyprus rode bicycles because taxis were expensive, and bus lines seldom got them to their destination.

At age 54 and 64, Diamondola and Aram decided to live like the Cypriots and ride bicycles. They didn't know what was in store for them the day they purchased their two-wheel monsters. Riding a bicycle looked simple enough; learning to ride one was another story. The wheel brakes stopped them too quickly, catapulting them headlong. They wobbled from side to side until one pedal eventually hit the ground, pitching them off sideways.

More bruises! They hit sidewalks, bumped off and skidded, depositing skin all over the cement. After practicing on the contrivances for five days, they limped to church on Sabbath. Fortunately, their clothing hid most of their battle scars and colorful bruises. Diamondola, who could hardly find a comfortable sitting position, envied Aram who could stand through the service while preaching.

Sunday began another period of torture. Finally, by the end of the week, the Ashods had mastered the art of riding a bicycle. Even pedestrians and other cyclists were now safe with Ashods on the street. Within the month, all bruises had healed, and Ashods had solved their transportation problem.

Ashods' public meetings were a disappointment to them—only a few attended. Aram spoke in either Armenian or Turkish, depending upon which group was in the majority that night; Diamondola translated into Greek. Some of the people, who seemed very interested in the message, suddenly stopped coming. The Ashods learned that the Armenian and Greek Orthodox priests had officially forbidden the people to go to any more Adventist meetings. Cyprus might be the land of the free, but few were brave enough to step out from their religious traditions.

Political unrest developed. Tension between the Greeks and Turks resulted in clashes. Fond hopes of an increased membership diminished, but Aram and Diamondola were not quitters. They continued to work, hoping some would be brave enough to accept the message.

* Barlas worked as a colporteur, Bible worker, preacher, or Correspondence School director for 41 years. In 1965 he went on sustentation but remained active by selling or giving away literature.

Chapter 24

LIVING AND LEAVING

The public meetings in Cyprus had not been a success. Ashods still clung to the hope that there would be some converts from their cottage meetings. Yonula, from whom they rented their duplex, was convinced of the truth, but her husband was adamantly opposed to her keeping the Sabbath. In spite of their diverse religious convictions, the two families remained the best of friends.

Yonula loved everyone and everything. One day she saw some boys playing with a partridge. "What are you going to do with the bird?" she asked them.

"Kill it and eat it," they answered.

Yonula couldn't stand the thought of the poor frightened bird becoming someone's snack, so she bought the bird from the boys. The partridge seemed to know that Yonula had saved him from the boiling pot. He followed her everywhere and became a household pet.

Ashods had acquired a kitten—by the kitten's choice, not theirs. It had followed them home from a walk and refused to leave. Ashods liked God's little creatures too, so they adopted it. The kitten and the partridge soon became good friends and played together in the garden shared by their owners. You would never see one without the other.

Diamondola put an old feather pillow in the hall porch for the cat to sleep on. The cat made a hollow spot in the middle of the pillow where she liked to sleep. Of course, the partridge had to sleep with the cat, so he snuggled up on the upper reaches of the pillow. Sometimes the partridge beat the cat to the hollow spot. This pushed hospitality a bit far. The kitten would walk around and around the pillow giving the bird big hints that it was time to move. If the bird didn't move, the cat begrudgingly lay down on the floor, placed his head on the pillow, and went to sleep beside the partridge.

The Ashods thoroughly enjoyed living on this island paradise. The food, climate, and people were great. Cyprus produced fruit and vegetables in abundance. The beaches were clean and sandy; the water was clear and warm. Camping in the mile-high Trodos Mountains surrounded by fragrant pines afforded relief from August's soaring temperatures. In the winter, the same mountains provided snow-covered slopes for skiing and sledding. The resort towns, snuggled along the southern shore of the island, provided restful retreats. Furthermore, Cyprus had a veritable treasury of archeological ruins to explore—Phoenician, Greek, Roman, Venetian, and Crusader.

When Indra came home from college that summer, there were a lot of places for the family to visit and enjoy. They purchased a bicycle for her, which she learned to ride without the physical damage her parents had suffered. They, with their friends, often took rides into the country. It was on one of these country excursions that Ashods and company met a camel driver with three adult camels and one baby. The man seemed lonely and anxious to talk to someone. On a small (40x140 miles) island, no one is in a hurry, so the Ashods obliged the man and sat down in the meadow to chat. For some ruminative reason, the baby camel took a liking to Diamondola and started examining her with his tongue. Now even a baby camel is a large animal compared to a four-foot, ten-inch lady. Spontaneously, Diamondola jumped to her feet and started to run from him. The baby camel trotted happily after her. Diamondola screamed and poured on the steam, her legs rotating like propellers. The young camel followed her at an easy gait. The long-legged quadruped had the advantage over the short-legged biped. Diamondola's "friends" stood on the sidelines, laughing their sides sore. It was like a circus—the baby camel running after a normally dignified, gray-haired lady, and the owner running to catch his camel. Just before the owner and Diamondola dropped from exhaustion, the owner caught the baby camel's halter.

"Why (puff) did you (puff) run from him (puff, puff)?" the owner asked.

"Because (puff) I was afraid (puff, PUFF)," Diamondola answered honestly, trying to blink her eye balls back into their sockets.

"He only wanted to play with you, Madam," the camel owner explained, still puffing heavily. "You are so little that he thought you were a human baby. He was just trying to be friendly—making sure you had a good time."

"Explain to him that I wasn't having a good time," Diamondola muttered, still gasping for air. She pointed to her companions who were still laughing and wiping their eyes. "Those are the ones having a good time. Just look at them! Please turn your adult camels loose on them so I can laugh, will you?"

Indra thoroughly enjoyed spending the summer of 1950 in Cyprus with her parents, Aunt Alexandra, and the grandmother whom she dearly loved. She couldn't remember home without grandmother. And, with the exception of Theodora's brief visit to Greece, neither could Diamondola. Her mother had lived with her since the death of her father in 1913. When Aram and Diamondola got married, Aram adopted Theodora as his mother, and she adopted him as the son she never had. The other daughters tried to nudge their mother away from the Ashods. Despina begged her mother to come to California to live with her. Susanna, whose husband was dead, wanted her mother's company in Greece. Despina and Susanna both thought it would be better for their mother to settle down in one comfortable place than to lead the nomadic life of missionary ambassadors, but Theodora knew what she wanted. "I will not leave Diamondola and my son Aram. I will travel with them wherever they go. If I die on the way, so be it. If I die in their place of labor, there will I be buried."

Mother Keanides was now nearly 95, and her body was weakening. Her mind was still as sharp as ever. She enjoyed having members of the family read to her. Indra spent many happy hours talking and reading to her "Yaya" (Greek for grandmother.)

Fall came and Indra left for Lebanon and Middle East College. The parting was hard since Indra feared she would never see her "Yaya" again on this earth.

But Grandmother waved her off with a smile. "We'll meet again. I'll race you to the Tree of Life, and you won't have to read to me there."

The autumn rains descended, and with them came the chilly weather. Theodora caught pneumonia. Her weak and tired body would not respond to treatment. She passed peacefully to her rest, believing with all her heart that God would resurrect her at His second coming.

Since they do almost no embalming in most Middle East countries, the law requires that the body be interred within 24 hours. The Ashods started burial procedures immediately, but they ran into unexpected difficulty. The Greek Orthodox Church refused to bury her in their cemetery since she was not a member of their church. The Armenian Orthodox refused interment since she was of Greek nationality. Finally, the British Military Cemetery officers graciously gave them a burial site between two English soldiers.

Theodora was known as "Mitera" (mother in Greek) by many whose lives she had touched. Ashods did not know how many friends she had made until they viewed the long funeral procession and saw her grave deluged with flowers. Laying mother in the grave was very difficult for the Ashods. She had always been a part of their family and work. It was hard to imagine life without her. Theodora's chair at the table was left in its place—empty.

But partings were not over. Soon after Christmas, Alexandra went to Susanna's home in Greece while she waited for Despina to arrange her financial guarantee for emigrating to the United States. Alexandra was 14 years older than Diamondola, and they understood her desire to get settled more comfortably. She had lived with them since 1941, so this leave-taking was also difficult. It was doubtful that they would ever see each other again.

During this period, China closed its borders to missionaries. An influx of overseas workers from the China Division arrived in the Middle East. The General Conference decided to organize the east Mediterranean countries into the Middle East Division of Seventh-day Adventists with headquarters in Beirut.* George Appel became the president and C. C. Morris the treasurer. The Adventists in the Bible lands felt blest by the added workers and funds. The division officers visited the entire field laying broad plans for expanding God's work.

Soon after the division officers left Cyprus, Ashods received word that they had been retired. Aram had spent 31 years in church work, and Diamondola 39 (not counting the times she had served as a translator in her childhood). Robert Mole took their place. They could see the wisdom in placing the administration of Cyprus in the hands of a younger man. They were satisfied with the decision of the division committee.

"Well, what do we do now, Diamondola?" Aram asked. His early retirement had come as a surprise, and he felt lost in the shuffle. "Where shall we go?"

"I'm still praying about it, but I feel impressed that we should go to Beirut where we can be near Indra. We have been active in Christian work all our lives, and there we can continue giving Bible studies and translating."

"That's true. Besides, Elder Hartwell did tell us that they will probably need someone who knows Armenian and Turkish in the Bible Correspondence School office in Beirut. I am concerned, however, that we won't be able to converse freely with most of the Lebanese. They speak Arabic, you know."

"Oh, we could learn Arabic like we have the other six languages. We learned Farsee, didn't we?" Diamondola reasoned. "Besides, Beirut is a metropolitan city with multi-lingual people. There's bound to be someone with whom we can study the Bible in Armenian, Greek, Turkish, French, German, or English."

From March to July the Ashods sorted out their belongings and finished their work in Cyprus. They had been there only two years, but they had put down roots and developed friendships.

"I must admit that I am getting weary of living in a place for awhile, learning to love it, and then leaving it," Diamondola sighed as she closed the lid of her suitcase.

Ashods sailed for Beirut on July 30, 1951. They planned that this would be their last move—they would never leave Lebanon.

* Cyprus was given mission status in 1953 with Fred Veltman as president. A church was built in Nicosia in 1956. Wayne Olson, ministerial secretary for Middle East Division, conducted an evangelistic series in the Ledra Palace Hotel in 1960. The results, as always in Cyprus, were almost nil. In 1964, civil strife between the Turks and Greeks on the island broke out in earnest. The church was looted and damaged by the Turks. It became a part of the Turkish sector when the island was divided. UN forces still keep the uneasy peace between the northern Turkish side and the southern Greek side of Cyprus.

During the re-organization of world divisions in the '70's, the Middle East lost its division status and became the Middle East Union. When civil war in Lebanon made it too difficult and dangerous for the leaders to move freely in and out of the country, the Middle East Union headquarters was moved from Beirut, Lebanon, to Nicosia, Cyprus. The Adventist membership in the Middle East remains small, especially since so many members and workers have fled to other countries. Even though the Middle East Union office is located in Cyprus, the membership there remains almost stagnant. Today (2004) _____ is president, and _____ is treasurer. The writer's son, David Olson, was a second generation missionary to the Middle East. He served there from 1985–1992 as assistant secretary/treasurer. His wife Cathy worked in the office. His children, Hans and Heidi, loved the island and the beaches. They still think of Cyprus as their childhood "home."

Chapter 25

LOVELY LEBANON

Aram and Diamondola stood by the ship's rail, watching the shoreline of beautiful Lebanon come into view. Light, sandy beaches merged into citrus, banana, and date palm groves. These were interlaced with year-around truck gardens. Beyond them rose the foothills covered with all varieties of fruit and nut trees, and umbrella pines. Higher up, the mountain ridges reached for the fleecy clouds floating in an azure dome. Sprinkled amid nature's masterpieces, and adding to the charm, were the limestone homes with red tile roofs, or cement-block houses tastefully painted and trimmed with colorful wood shutters and balconies.

"'The glory of Lebanon shall come to you, the pine, the fir, and the cypress together,'" Diamondola quoted from Isaiah. "Oh, Aram, this truly is a beautiful land that we have chosen as our last earthly abode."

"It certainly looks inviting, and I'm sure we will find plenty to do here. Now I just hope our sustentation money will be sufficient for our needs."

"No need to worry about money here. Beirut is one of the world's largest banking centers; we should be able to get all the money we need," Diamondola joked. "I'm going to deposit my $25 savings to draw interest."

"Okay, Diamondola, enough of your humor," Aram said, changing the subject. "You see those modern high-rise buildings? They're indicative of a flourishing economy. Lebanon is the gem of the Mediterranean, the Switzerland of the Middle East, but even in this paradise, nothing is free. This is Lebanon—not heaven." The ship docked; Indra and her friends were there to meet them. They whisked the Ashods off to Middle East College. There they stayed with Edith Davis and Aram's niece, Shahin Ilter, until they could find housing. They would have liked to live on Jebel Sebtia (Adventist Mountain) where they would be near Indra, but, outside of the college buildings, there was no housing within a mile or more. Even the Middle East College property was still in its developmental stages. Faculty and students had moved into the incompleted dormitory buildings only four years earlier—the fall of 1947. The spring on the college property gave only a trickle of water and was insufficient for the students' use. No one would build on the hill until a dependable water source was available.

Ashods finally found an apartment they could afford in the Mouseitbe area, Moslem West Beirut. The Adventist school, church, and Bible Correspondence School offices were located only a few blocks from Ashods home. The Moslems were good neighbors, but there was one drawback that kept the Ashods feeling isolated from the crowd—everyone spoke Arabic, and that was a language they didn't know.

The day came when the Ashods and their goods met at their not-so-new, but sufficiently modern, apartment. As they unpacked, a shroud of loneliness enveloped them. For the first time in their married lives, just the two of them would be in the house—no Theodora, Indra, Alexandra, orphans, or refugees. They tried to drown these lonely feelings by pitching right into the work of arranging the house. By 3 p.m. everything was in place, and they felt starved.

Diamondola went to the hole-in-the-wall grocery store around the corner. The one-man operation did not offer much variety. "Eggs, bread, cheese, and oil," Diamondola told the proprietor in all six of her spoken languages. He shrugged his shoulders; he didn't understand her. She finally resorted to pointing to all the items except the eggs. She couldn't see them anywhere. She formed the shape of an egg with her hands. The good-natured owner tried to figure out what she meant. Oranges? Pomegranates? Apples? Diamondola shook her head. In desperation she crowed like a rooster and said "mama." The Lebanese grocer burst into laughter when he realized that she wanted the fruit of the mama rooster. He pulled a basket of eggs from under the counter, and Diamondola selected the number she wanted. She handed him a fist full of Lebanese currency, and he sorted out what he needed. Diamondola and the grocer never did learn to speak each other's languages, but they did business from then on with signs that only they understood.

Before retirement blues had a chance to settle on Aram, he was asked to translate the Bible Correspondence lessons into Turkish and Armenian. In no time the lessons were published and sent out to interested students. Aram then corrected and returned the lessons. Now he was happy. The salary as a part-time employee relieved their financial squeeze.

Ashods planned to attend the Mouseitbe Arabic Church since getting to the English services up at the college was like a journey of a hundred miles and very time consuming. The first Sabbath in Mouseitbe, Diamondola was elated to be sitting in a real church until the service began. Then she whispered to Aram, "Wouldn't you know it? When I'm finally privileged to attend an honest-to-goodness Seventh-day Adventist church instead of meeting in a home or a basement, I can't understand a thing that's going on. It's a good thing I have my Sabbath School quarterly and Bible along."

Toward the end of the service, Diamondola rested her eyes and gazed about at the members. Her eyes fastened on a man who looked vaguely familiar. After church she singled him out. "Dikran!" she called as she ran to the man she recognized as the inspiration of her childhood days. After tears of joy and Christian embraces, they recalled their days in Turkey. Diamondola had been only a child then, and Dikran a young man. He came to their home in Brousa for Sabbath services. In order to spend the Sabbath hours with fellow believers, Dikran left his home Friday evening and walked the 35 miles to Brousa. After lunch, Dikran held Diamondola and Despina spellbound with stories of Sabbath-keeping difficulties he had experienced with his father and his boss. He related the details of his beatings and imprisonment for distributing literature. The young sisters wondered if they would ever be able to survive trials such as Dikran had endured. In 1906, Dikran left the Brousa area and worked as a colporteur. During the deportations, he had managed to escape to Beirut. Here, after 45 years, Diamondola and Dikran meet again. What thrilling evenings the Dikran and Ashod families spent reminiscing and recounting the goodness of God who had preserved them through years of persecution in Turkey when millions of Christians perished. Now Dikran's children, Rose, Angel, and Evelyn, were already Adventist teachers, and Indra was preparing herself to be useful to the church they all loved.

The Ashods purchased an Arabic grammar book and set about learning the language. After several months, Diamondola plunked her grammar book down on the table. "Aram, I'm getting nowhere with this stuff. Either I'm too old to learn a new language, or my brain is too full to absorb any more."

"I've got the same trouble. I'll never be able to enjoy a sermon in Arabic. Let's give up and go to the English church services up at the college. That way we can see Indra, Shakee, Shaheen, and Edith once a week, and benefit from a worship service we can understand."

But getting up to the college was a very complicated, five-mile excursion across town and up the hill. First, they had to take a service taxi—one that runs a certain route like a city bus—down to the hub of the city. From there they caught another service taxi out to Dekouane, a suburb at the bottom of the Adventist Mountain. Then they walked the mile and a half up the hill to the college, arriving there in time for Sabbath School.

Sabbaths became Ashods high day of the week. They became acquainted with the foreign Adventist missionaries. They had great fun being with the girls, and Edith and Shahin were ever the perfect hostesses. In fact, they enjoyed themselves so much they often stayed for the evening program. Then they had a difficult time getting home. First, they had to walk to the bottom of the hill in the dark with howling jackals following them. Getting a taxi from Dekouane into the hub of the city was usually impossible since the taxis stopped running at sundown. That forced them to take the real scary route—the three and a half mile trek through the asphalt jungle of Beirut to Mouseitbe. This five-mile midnight hike from the college to Mouseitbe would have challenged the courage and fortitude of brave youth, but Diamondola and Aram (now in their 60's and 70's) did it regularly. As God's ambassadors in the Middle East, boldness had become ingrained in their make-up. The couple talked and sang as they hurried through dark alleys and dimly lit streets until they reached their Mouseitbe apartment. "Safe at home again," Diamondola sighed as she flopped into her rocker.

"My hair, which has been standing at attention, can now lay back down. Every time we start that shortcut from Dekouane to Mouseitbe, I promise myself that I will never stay late at the college again. But then the next Sabbath when I get up to the college, temptation overcomes me again. I pray God they'll find water up there soon; then people can start building apartment houses on the hill."

"Small chance! Wishful thinking!" Aram sighed as he mopped the perspiration from his forehead. "Before that happens we'll be dead."

"It doesn't hurt to dream," Diamondola said as she kicked the oxfords off her sore feet. "Maybe someday…"

Chapter 26

MOVING UP

The Middle East Division finally solved the lack-of-water problem for Middle East College. The Division purchased a small farm at the foot of the hill where they dug a good well and pumped the water a mile up to storage tanks at the college. With water available, the mission could now develop more fully their 70- acre plot. They added a few faculty homes and hired Cliff Dinning to build Middle East Press on a corner of the college property. This was the first mission owned printing press in the Middle East! The Ashods, who had probably done more translation and editorial work for the church than anyone else, were thrilled with this advancement.

Ashods were even more thrilled when Dinning asked Aram to join their staff as full-time editor for the Armenian and Turkish publications. During the years Aram worked at the press, he translated and published the *Week of Prayer Readings, Bedtime Stories, The Impending Conflict, Training Light Bearers, The Marked Bible, Better Living, the Armenian Song Book* (to which Aram added 25 new hymns), the first half of *Desire of the Ages*, and revised *Steps to Christ*.

Aram was in his element at the press, and the full-time wages helped with their bills and Indra's tuition. Transportation up to the press during the week was quite simple. A group of press workers from Mouseitbe hired a taxi each day to take them directly to and from the college hill. Sabbath transportation, however, was still a problem for Ashods.

Since Aram's work had moved from the Bible Correspondence School in Mouseitbe up to the press, the Ashods prayed more earnestly than ever that they might find housing near the college hill. Soon that prayer was answered. A casual acquaintance called at their home to tell them that he had purchased land just below Middle East Press where he planned to build an apartment complex. He asked Ashods if they wanted to reserve one of the six apartments. Ashods were definitely interested, but before they signed a lease, they had the foresight to ask about the water situation. The builder assured them that he had arranged for Dekouane city water to be pumped up to his building. Then Ashods agreed to rent an apartment at a designated price.

The Ashods were euphoric when, after a few months, the building was completed, and the owner gave them an occupancy date. Ashods in turn gave their Mouseitbe landlord notice that they would be moving. The landlord promptly found new tenants for Ashods' apartment. The night before the move, however, the owner of the hill property informed Ashods that their apartment rent would be a sum considerably more than he had quoted to them originally. They could not afford to pay this amount and reminded the owner of his agreement. But the owner simply shrugged his shoulders and left. Ashods were heartsick. For months they had counted on living close to Aram's work in order to save him the effort and expense of commuting. Now they had no place to go since the Mouseitbe rental had already been leased to someone else.

Ashods prayed through the night reminding the Lord of this crises they faced. They were tempted to feel bitter against the apartment owner who had deceived them. But they remembered that God had solved bigger problems than this for them.

The next day they begged a few days reprieve from the new renters of their Mouseitbe apartment. It was granted. Then they hunted all day for some housing at the foot of the college hill, but they found nothing. They prayed some more. Their few possessions were setting about the house in boxes, just waiting to be moved—somewhere—anywhere.

The next day Aram found himself walking up the winding asphalt road to the college. Every little while he stopped in the shade of the umbrella pines, wiped away the tears of despondency running down his cheeks, and talked some more to God. He dropped down onto a large stone that was of comfortable sitting size to consider their plight. Why had their well-laid plans gone awry? And why was he, Aram, on the college hill during the heat of the day, anyway? This was even a mystery to Aram himself. He supposed it was his way of mitigating the agony.

He eased himself off the stone to continue his trek up the hill when suddenly a car screeched to a stop beside him. It was Wadie Farag, one of the teachers from Middle East College.

"Hi, Brother Ashod," called Wadie congenially. "Looks like you need a ride. Get in and I'll take you wherever you're going." Aram greeted Wadie and climbed into the car. "How're you doing?" Wadie continued pleasantly.

"Not so good. It's like this…" and Aram spilled the whole sad tale of their predicament to Wadie, whom he knew was a good listener.

"You are in a mean situation," Wadie sympathized. "We can't let you and Sister Ashod be put out on the streets, now can we? I've got an idea. Hear me out and agree. I am a bachelor with a large apartment at the bottom of the hill. It could easily accommodate you folks and me. It would be relatively convenient for you because, like Moses, your strength has not waned. You could easily walk the mile and a half up the hill to the press each day, couldn't you?"

Aram nodded.

"Well, then, that's settled. Let's go get your things and move you into my place until something opens up for you." Wadie spoke as if there were no choice. "I'll move into the small bedroom, and you two can have the large one. You can spread your things wherever you want in the rest of the house."

Aram could hardly believe this generous offer. Big-hearted Wadie had an immediate solution to their dilemma and at some inconvenience to himself. But that was Wadie. Had it been anyone else, the Ashods would have hesitated to accept such a magnanimous proposal.

Before the day was over, Wadie had moved Ashods' household effects into his apartment. By evening, Diamondola was settled and preparing dinner for the men. "You are the fastest answer to prayer I've ever seen," Diamondola said becoming a little teary. "How can we ever thank you, Wadie? No son could have been better to us than you have been today."

Wadie brushed off the compliment with a wave of his hand, "It's nothing. Just doing what the early Christians did for one another."

Ashods learned how hospitable Wadie really was during the next few months. He always acted as if they were doing him a favor by occupying his apartment. After four months, the owner of the apartment complex near the college came to Ashods with a new proposal. He had not been able to rent the apartments at the higher price. Now he offered to split the difference between his original price and the higher one. The Ashods signed the contract and moved up on the hill.

Ashods' dream of living near the college had materialized, but there was an annoyance—the owner had not been able to purchase sufficient water rights to adequately supply his six apartments. The college itself had the water they needed from the farm well at the foot of the hill, but they wouldn't dare venture into the business of selling water. The legal aspects were too sticky. In the Middle East, water is like a gold commodity.

"I've got the solution to our meager water supply," Diamondola informed her husband. "I'll take a bath one day and you the next. We'll save the bath water for flushing toilets and washing the floors. Only cooking and drinking water can't be "used" water. Laundry may be a problem, but we'll manage."

Eventually the owner put a storage reservoir on the roof for each apartment. The water would drip into the reservoir all day and night, keeping it fairly well filled. Ashods were thankful for the reservoir because they needed more water when Indra left the dormitory to live with them.

Grocery shopping was their most vexing problem. The Ashods had to walk all the way to the bottom of the hill, buy what they could carry, and walk back up the hill. Eventually the college built a store and bakery which solved that inconvenience.

While Indra was busy in school and Aram at the press, Diamondola was busy being "Mrs. Dorcas" for the needy college students and the poor of the community. She also spent several days a week in the city giving Bible studies to French and German-speaking people. In fact, Diamondola was so busy she scarcely allowed herself time to miss her deceased mother and her three sisters.

One day a letter arrived from Despina. It read: "How would you like to have company? I am in Europe visiting my daughter, Dorothy. Her husband, Dr. Howard Conley, is currently stationed here with the U.S. forces. Dorothy and I will go to Beirut, and Susanna says she will come there from Greece. I can hardly wait to see you. We three sisters will have a great reunion while the cousins, Dorothy and Indra, get acquainted.

Diamondola dropped the letter and went into orbit. Never had she imagined she would see Despina and Susanna in this world again. It had been over 30 years since their heart-breaking separation in Istanbul when the authorities had refused to give Despina permission to leave the boat. No one could stop this reunion!

When the guests arrived, the three sisters made use of every precious minute—talking, touching, remembering. How they wished their beloved spinster sister Alexandra could have been with them too. Alexandra lived frugally in Greece on her sustentation check. The sisters agreed among themselves that Alexandra was getting too old to care for herself. When the reunion was over, Despina sent the papers and money to bring Alexandra to live with her in California. The next year, 1955, Susanna's eldest son in the States sent for his mother and his younger brother Pano and his family. Now all of the family except Diamondola, Aram, and Indra lived near one another in California. At times, Diamondola gave in to self pity and cried, wishing so much she could be near the rest of the family. But she knew deep down within her that this would never be.

Diamondola consoled herself by visiting with those about her. Living in their apartment complex were some of the best family members she could ever want. They were an international family of Seventh-day Adventists. Across the hall from them lived Wadie Farag, Egyptian, and his bride, Dola Hasso, Swiss/Iraqi. Downstairs lived the Rices, Indian and Armenian; the Haddads, Lebanese; Faimanns, Austrian and Palestinian; and the Antars, Iraqi. The families used English as their medium of communication. There was always someone around—except when you really needed them.

One day Aram set fire to some trash on the edge of the apartment property. A slight wind whipped the fire through the dead pine needles and then swept it up toward the press building. No one answered Aram's clarion call for help except Indra and Diamondola. They formed a bucket brigade and worked furiously to smother the flames. Then they stamped out the smoldering embers with their feet. After it was over, they dragged their weary frames up the steps to their apartment. They were wet, dirty, exhausted, and smelled of smoke. Diamondola flopped into a chair. "The next time you burn trash, Aram, make sure the whole apartment crowd is on hand to enjoy your sport of fire fighting."

Anees Haddad, one of the neighbors, was the dynamic youth leader for Middle East Division. "Sister Ashod, work on your

Master Guide class and be invested with Indra. You can easily do it," urged Mr. Psychology.

So Diamondola hiked, studied astronomy, flowers, trees—THE WORKS! She struggled to complete the courses; Diamondola was not a quitter. Theodore Lucas came from the General Conference of Seventh-day Adventists in Washington, D.C., for the Investiture Service and honored Diamondola as the oldest candidate. "And getting invested has aged this Mistress Guide ten years," Diamondola mumbled, glad that it was over.

After graduating from the academy, Indra took two years of secretarial training at the college. She went to work for Elder Hartwell in the Union Office. She worked for a little over a year; then the Lebanese government refused to renew her work permit because she was a Turkish citizen. "How ironic!" remarked Diamondola. "Christians have a hard time finding professional jobs in Moslem Turkey. Then when we move to a Christian country, we can't work because we are Turkish. I'll be so thankful to get to heaven where we won't need passports, visas, or work permits. I can pass through the pearly gates without flashing my I.D. card, and Gabriel won't ask to see my work permit before I tend my vineyard."

Indra's aggravation was a blessing in disguise. She went back to college and took the education courses she had always wanted. This detour would open doors full of happy surprises. She began by teaching secondary classes at Middle East College—Bible, biology, English, and general science.

Ashods spent a great deal of time encouraging, entertaining, and helping college students who came from distant countries, especially those from Turkey and Iran. They became particularly attached to Shapoor Ansari, a shy, polite freshman from Iran. He shared his concerns for his family with them. His father was old and not well; his mother, the youngest of his Moslem father's three wives, was mistreated by his father's older sons and their mothers. Their contempt for her increased when she became a Christian while recovering from childbirth in a Christian

145

hospital. Mr. Ansari was understanding of his wife's religious preference, and even sent Shapoor to attend the Iran Adventist Training School near Teheran.

Upon completing high school, Shapoor begged to go to Middle East College with his friends. His father agreed and paid his way. But before the year was over, Shapoor got word that his father had died suddenly. His older, full brother in the States sent word for Shapoor to go to Iran immediately and arrange to send their mother to him. He knew that the other wives and children would be standing about like vultures, waiting to gobble up all the inheritance. Shapoor's mother and her sons should receive their share of the inheritance legally; but even if they didn't get anything from their father's property, they would be quite well off. Their mother's father had given her a large dowry and a nice piece of land when she married. According to law, this dowry remained in her name and/or that of her children forever. When Shapoor arrived home, however, he found his mother in a most pitiful condition. She was just a sick, starving pauper holed up in a ratty room. "What happen to you, Mother?" he cried upon seeing her in rags.

"The other wives and their sons threw me out of my own home and confiscated all my property—clothes, jewels, furniture, house, lands, EVERYTHING. With bribes and fraud they have taken all of my inheritance. How all of the legal deeds and papers could disappear or be written in their names is no mystery. The government officers and lawyers have been well paid to make the fraud worth their while. There is no mercy or justice for us here. Let's hurry and leave Iran before they kill us."

Shapoor knew this could happen. Getting rid of them would eliminate any legal battles for the greedy relatives. Shapoor sold the few jewels his mother had sneaked from her home by concealing them under her clothing. With the money, he purchased bus tickets for Beirut. But the stress of the past few months had taken its toll; before they could leave, Mrs. Ansari had a serious stroke. This complicated their bus trip. Shapoor had to carry his mother into all of the rest stops, feed her, and take her to the toilet. The other passengers admired the loving care Shapoor gave his mother and helped him when they could.

Somehow, the Ansaris managed to travel the 1100 miles overland to Beirut. They found a cheap hotel near the American Embassy and began working on her emigration papers. Soon it was evident that it would be a long time before the embassy would end its investigation and issue papers for Mrs. Ansari. They were out of money and out on the street before Shapoor's pride would allow him to contact his friends. The Ashods insisted that Shapoor and his mother come to them. Before the Ansaris arrived, Ashods' wonderful neighbors determined to share in the missionary endeavor. Antars let the refugees have an empty apartment rent-free. Other Adventists loaned sufficient furniture to make the place livable. Then they began around-the-clock nursing and restaurant services. Rices, Antars, and Ashods all shared in the cooking, cleaning, washing, and care of the patient while Shapoor worked. They bathed and exercised Mrs. Ansari; they carried her outdoors for fresh air; they took her to the doctor; they bought her medicine and made sure she took it. One of the Ashods always had to be on hand to translate because Mrs. Ansari could speak only a slurred Farsee. Gradually the stroke victim improved in health and spirits. Their TLC was effective.

School began again. One of the married couples cottages became available, and Shapoor and his mother moved there. She was pleased when she was well enough to move herself about by leaning on a chair and pushing it in front of her. She did her own cooking and cleaning, and others helped her with the laundry.

One day Diamondola asked this sweet, illiterate woman how she learned to believe in Jesus. "Oh," she answered simply, "when I heard about Jesus, I knew He was God because He rose from the grave and went to heaven. I pray to Jesus, and He does everything for me. His people are kind and loving too. Without you Christians, I would be dead; and without Jesus, I would die eternally."

A number of months later Shapoor and his mother got their papers and left to live with the older brother in Washington, D. C. Mrs. Ansari lived only a few more years, but died knowing that she would live again.

The Ansaris were gone, but Diamondola knew that soon there would be someone else needing her attention.

"Ah," Diamondola sighed contentedly as she sat on her balcony watching the setting sun cast ripples of gold on the vast expanse of the blue Mediterranean Sea. "These past seven years in Lebanon have been absolutely divine. Aram has contributed his talents to the publishing work. I've seen results from my Bible studies. Together we've given Christian care to many people who needed it, and all the while, we've enjoyed the peace, beauty, and tranquility of lovely Lebanon. Moving up to the college hill has been like moving just a little closer to heaven."

Chapter 27

AMBASSADORS TRAVEL

Aram sat in his favorite rocker reading to Diamondola who was curled up on the davenport. "'God, whom I serve with all my heart in preaching the gospel of His Son, is my witness how constantly I remember you in my prayers at all times; and I pray that now at last by God's will the way may be opened for me to come to you. I long to see you so that I may impart to you some spiritual gift to make you strong—that you and I may be mutually encouraged by each other's faith.' Paul wrote that in Romans 1: 9–12. You know, Diamondola, I feel just like the apostle did."

"That's good," Diamondola murmured through a big yawn. She stretched and tucked a throw pillow under her head. "Paul was a good man."

"Diamondola, pay attention!" Aram remonstrated. "I'm trying to make a point. What is Paul saying in those verses?"

"Oh, I guess he's telling those to whom he preached the gospel that he prays for them a lot and would like to see them again so that they could encourage one another. See there, Aram. I was listening!" Diamondola gave the pillow another punch and dropped back onto its softness.

"Granted. But I still want to pick your brain about an idea I've been toying with lately. We get so many letters from old friends to whom we preached the gospel. I, like Paul, would like to see them one last time so that we can encourage one another."

"That would be nice," Diamondola rolled over and closed her eyes.

"So, I thought I'd ask for a three-months leave from work, and we'll spend the summer going to Iraq, Iran, and Turkey visiting the members and…"

Like a shot from a cannon, Diamondola was off the davenport and facing Aram.

"You mean we'll take a three-month holiday and travel around the Middle East seeing friends?"

"Take it easy, my Dear! You startled me so much I nearly rocked over backwards," Aram chided. "And lower your voice. I declare it only takes a few words to trip your adventure button."

"How perfectly splendificent! When can we leave? Where will we go first?" The words tumbled from Diamondola's mouth in staccato.

"Whoa! Calm down, Diamondola, and just listen. I thought we'd make a circuit through Iraq, Iran, into Turkey and then back here. First I must get approval for my three-months leave, next comes the visas, then exchange our money into foreign currency, and…"

"And I'll prepare some emergency food rations, pack the suitcases, and oh, yes, I must get a notebook for my journal. I'll entitle it THE AMBASSADORS' SUMMER OF 1960." Diamondola smiled exuberantly, folded her hands demurely, and looked for all the world like she was ready for translation.

"Well, get a big notebook. If I know you, Diamondola, you will fill a volume. You have a stack of diaries now that you've kept since you were 16."

"I know," Diamondola condescended. "In them I have a permanent, accurate record of all that has gone on in our fields of labor."

It is doubtful that Diamondola slept much that night. The prospects of an extended vacation, which would take them back through memory's lane, kept her on an emotional high.

Aram was granted his leave of absence; visas were secured in a remarkably short time; and friends they hoped to visit were contacted. They stuffed a few gifts into their suitcases, and they put money and traveler's checks into their pockets. Then they were off for Basra, Iraq, to see Berjouhi, the young lady in Istanbul who had the dream about seeing Aram preach.

Basra had so few members it was hard for them to keep up their courage. They didn't have a pastor, and seldom did they even get a visit from the mission president. The ten-day sojourn of Aram and Diamondola pumped new hope into the whole membership. During those days the Ashods had Sabbath and evening meetings and fed them spiritually just like Paul would have done for his converts.

The temperatures at Basra soared above the 120 degree mark daily, melting the asphalt on the streets. People joked that gravel had to be poured on the asphalt streets to keep them from trickling into the sea.

The day before they were to leave Basra, a terrible dust storm blew in from the desert. Fine yellow dust filtered into the houses covering everything. In the morning when Diamondola arose, she dug dust from her ears, wiped dirt from her lips and grit from her teeth. After she had coughed her lungs clear, she took one look at Aram and exploded into hysterical laughter. "Oh, Aram you look hideous! You're all yellow! Except your eyes."

"Look in the mirror, Madam. What is your color?"

Diamondola wiped the fine particles of yellow sand from the mirror and looked. "Yep! You're right. Yellow doesn't suit me either."

The storm lasted two more days, causing the Ashods to cancel their trip to southern Iran. Berjouhi felt it was God's gift of love to the Basra members—it gave them two more days with God's ambassadors.

Ashods boarded the train for Teheran. Their budget limited them to third class coach chairs. They had to sit up day and night, taking their food and water with them. This they did not mind, but the heat and dust were most oppressive. One slept while the other guarded their property from the ever-present thieves. They had budgeted their money for this trip very carefully and couldn't risk the chance of being robbed. Diamondola suggested that she carry all of the papers and most of the currency in her purse. Aram agreed that would be the safest way to carry their valuables, so the transfer was made.

They arrived in Teheran safely with their two large suitcases, food basket, and water jug. They got off the train and bargained for a taxi to take them to the mission. They struck a deal with a driver and got in his taxi. But then, when he reneged on his word and quoted them an exorbitant price, they asked him to let them out. A second taxi driver stepped up and offered to take them at the going rate, so they got into his cab. The two drivers squabbled over the business of "stealing patrons." The second man finally drove off leaving the first one shaking his fists.

They were excited as they drove into the mission compound. Gladys Skinner, wife of the mission president, welcomed them into her cool living room. What a relief to get away from the hassle of the train, the heat, and the quarreling taxi drivers. While Gladys went to arrange one of the children's rooms for the Ashods to stay in, Bob Skinner and Aram carried the luggage in from the veranda. Then the four relaxed on wicker sofas and drank cool, refreshing lemonade while they chatted. Suddenly Diamondola sat bolt upright. "Aram! My purse! My purse is missing! In my weariness I must have left it in the taxi!!"

They made a hurried search. The purse was definitely missing. All their travel documents and most of their money was GONE. They knelt right down and prayed that God would help them find the purse. Then the men rushed back into the city to try to find the taxi drivers and report the loss to the police. While they were gone, Gladys tried to get Diamondola to freshen up, take a bath, and change into some clean clothes. But Diamondola could not be convinced to do anything but stay right there in the living room and pray.

The devil kept tempting Diamondola to think that the trip was not God's will, that their loss of money was God's way of punishing them. Diamondola's thoughts kept vacillating between remorse and hope. After an hour of mental anguish, she finally put the devil in his place—"Get behind me."

Aram and Bob returned from the city looking like defeated politicians. Diamondola could tell by the tightly-drawn lines in Aram's face that he was worried. He tried to relieve Diamondola's mind by saying, "Don't worry, my Dear. We'll borrow money and return directly to Beirut."

"But I've spoiled our wonderful trip—the one we anticipated and planned with such pleasure," Diamondola sobbed. "It was my idea to put the money in my purse. I left that purse somewhere. It's all my fault!" Nothing anyone said could console Diamondola. Aram went to take his bath. He left Diamondola pacing the floor and talking to God. "I guess this was presumptuous of us to take this journey believing You wanted us to comfort and encourage the believers. Probably we should have made a pleasure trip to Europe instead. Please God, what we need now is a miracle. A MIRACLE!"

While Diamondola was pacing the floor, praying and crying, Skinners little boy came running into the parlor. "Mrs. Ashod, two men are at the door to see you," he said.

Diamondola flew down the steps to greet the men. There stood the two drivers with her purse demanding 200 tumans for its return. She told them to please wait a moment and her husband would be down to consult with them. While they waited for Aram to come downstairs, she asked the men where they had found her purse. The first man said that after Ashods left his taxi, a nicely dressed man came along and asked to be taken only a short distance. He found Diamondola's purse and told the driver to find the owner and take it to her. Then he warned the driver that he had taken down his taxi number and would report this information to the police. So the first taxi driver had to find the second taxi driver to find out where he had taken the Ashods. By the time they finished their story, Aram had finished dressing.

Aram greeted the men, took the purse, and examined its contents. He looked at the men suspiciously, "Almost all of the U. S. dollars and English pounds are missing. You go and get them, then I'll give you a reward. If not, I must report you to the police."

The men looked sheepishly at each other. The one said, "Let's go back and find the man who gave us the purse. Maybe he kept some of the money."

Soon the two returned with all the English currency, but not much U. S. money. "I want the U.S. money back too," Aram demanded.

The men became angry and told him, "We have returned all the money the man would give us. You didn't have more money than that. Now give us our reward!"

"Ah," Aram said, "that is where you are mistaken. Look here at this paper. This is the declaration of currency that I reported on my passport. It was recorded and ratified at the border when I entered Iran. You cannot deny this statement of your officials."

Entangled in their deceit, the men agreed to "go back and see the man again."

Momentarily they were back with the rest of the money—which, of course, they had extracted from their own pockets once they were outside the mission wall.

Aram gave the men a big reward, and they went off happy, arm in arm. Ashods set aside a big thank offering for the Lord too. They wondered if the man the first driver had picked up for the short trip was an angel. In any case, that man had been careful to give detailed instructions to the driver, forcing him to return the purse from fear of the police.

The Ashods spent a number of days in Teheran visiting friends and encouraging the believers. The Skinners were gracious hosts, even inviting people to their house to see the Ashods.

From Teheran they went to Isfahan where they spent happy times reminiscing with Kristin and Gabriel. The next stop was Tabriz. There they met the Salakians again. In Riziah they found the Bible worker, Nanajan, still working energetically and single-handedly in that city. Her health was poor since she had had tuberculosis. It had affected her throat; she could only speak in a whisper. Yet it was she who kept the small membership together.

They returned to Teheran and took the bus to Baghdad. They were pleased to see the beautiful new church* in the city. The Iraqi Adventists supported the church with generous offerings and had no need for outside financial help—a rare case in point for most foreign fields.

Two months of the Ashods' wonderful vacation was over. They spent the next month in Turkey. They stayed with Kevork Yeshil's mother and younger brother. They were pleased to see that Kevork was a leading member in the church. And speaking of CHURCHES! One of Ashods' dreams had been realized—the Adventists now owned their own church in Istanbul! One of Kevork's influential friends helped the Adventists get permission to build the first Christian church in Turkey since the beginning of World War I. Conrad Rasmussen, mission president in those days, and Kevork set about immediately to complete the building before something happened to stop the miracle from becoming a reality. The Moslem government** had been very good to them, and the members appreciated the favor. The church was squeezed into a very narrow piece of land behind the mission house—just where Aram had always wanted to build one. Worshipping in an Adventist church in Istanbul was the greatest event of the whole summer for the Ashods.***

The three months missionary journey to encourage and fellowship with the believers was over. When the Ashods got back to Beirut, Diamondola wrote on the last page of her diary, "Home at last. The next trip to see our converts will be free. With heaven our destination, we won't need passports or money; no thieves will disturb our tranquility; no dust storms or heat waves will cause us discomfort. Bliss—eternal bliss—for us, your children. Thank you, Jesus."

*Some may question the advisability of our people investing money in church buildings in a Moslem country. For the most part, Adventists and Moslems live harmoniously. Neither religion believes in having images in their churches or mosques. The Moslems, like the Adventists, are against the use of pork, alcohol, drugs, and tobacco. Adventists do not enter into politics, so they are no threat to internal security. Therefore, Adventists are generally accepted and appreciated by the Moslem governments.

** The Turkish government today should not be compared to that of yesteryears when Ashods lived there.

***At the time of Ashods' visit to Turkey, the Curtis Miller and the Manoug Benzatian families were in charge of the work there.

Chapter 28

EDUCATION WITH A BONUS

Indra raced up the steps to her parents' apartment and burst through the door. "Guess what?" she said, quite out of breath. "The college president called me into his office today and suggested that I go to Emmanuel Missionary College in Berrien Springs, Michigan, for two years to get my master's degree."

Aram laid down his paper and peered over the top of his glasses. "My dear child, I wish I hadn't heard that. You already have your college degree and a good teaching job here. Two years is a long time. Your mother and I would miss you terribly."

"Don't worry, Daddy," Indra said as she bent over his rocker and placed a kiss on her father's forehead, "I'm not the least bit interested in going. In fact, I'm not going to go unless God becomes quite direct about it." As she ran her fingers through his wavy hair, she noticed that it was graying a lot faster lately. "Eventually, I will need to get my master's degree since Middle East College hopes to affiliate with Loma Linda University in California, but I can get it at the American University of Beirut."

"You'll do no such thing, Indra," Diamondola objected as she walked in from the kitchen drying her hands on her apron. "I don't want you going to a worldly university. I'd rather miss you for two years." Turning to Aram she added, "She'll be back before we know it."

"I suppose she should go to EMC, but when someone leaves this country they almost never return. I couldn't bear not to see

157

Indra again," Aram said with a catch in his throat and a tear in his eye.

For the next few days, Indra prayed that God would show her the direction she should take. It was with a twinge of sorrow that she finally accepted God's answer—"Go to the States."

By September all of Indra's documents were ready and her plane tickets purchased. Indra was happy that she would not travel to Michigan alone—a young man from Middle East College had also enrolled at EMC. They could fly together from Beirut to South Bend, Indiana. However, at the last minute the young man decided to stay over in London to see his brother before continuing on to the United States. Indra was very apprehensive about making the second leg of the journey alone, but she chose to stick with the original plans and scheduled flights.

Shortly before midnight, September 14, 1961, Indra and her parents huddled together at the Beirut airport. All the bravado the three mustered could not submerge the inner emotions that must eventually surface for expression. The parting was painful. The Ashods had experienced too many goodbyes that were forever. They held Indra tightly, too full of grief for words. Then they kissed for the last time, and Indra disappeared through the passenger gate. The Ashods went back to their empty apartment, hoping, praying that God would bring them together again.

In a few days they received Indra's cable. "Arrived safely. Am with Aunt Despina in California. Letter follows."

"CALIFORNIA!?!" Aram exclaimed aghast. "She's supposed to be in Michigan! I can't believe this. Here you read it, Diamondola. My eyes must be playing tricks on me."

Diamondola studied the cable. "No, Aram, I'm afraid you're right. Whatever could have happened? Now I'm worried," Diamondola fumed. "I hope there's a good explanation for the drastic change in her plans."

It seemed like eons before Indra's letter arrived. When it did, Aram tore open the envelope and handed it to Diamondola. "Hurry and read it. I'm about to suffocate with suspense."

Excerpts from Indra's letter dated September 18 read, "I'm sure you were surprised to hear that I am in California (an understatement)...I had a pleasant trip...I arrived in London safely and Alitalia Airlines took good care of me...sent me to a hotel to rest. After lunch they took me back to my plane bound for New York...I wasn't sick at all, which wasn't the fault of the airline—they fed me every 45 minutes, I believe."

"Diamondola, please skim down to the California part and omit the trivia for now. My curiosity is KILLING me," Aram said impatiently.

"Alright. Ah, the weather, food, ah," Diamondola mumbled as she glanced through the letter. "Here it is! 'When I got off the plane in New York, someone handed me a telegram from Aunt Despina urging me to go to her in California, but I had settled on EMC so asked Alitalia to put me on the plane for South Bend. They told me they had gotten me to New York and had no more responsibility for me. I put up quite an argument, Daddy. You would have been proud of me. I told them the agent in Beirut had promised that their agent in New York would get me on the right plane for Michigan. But there was no plane out to South Bend that night. I was truly distraught by this time. I prayed and felt impressed to call Aunt Despina. She urged me to hop a plane immediately for California saying that the education there was every bit as good as at EMC. Since there was a plane out to California that night, I got on it. My heart kept reminding me that my good friends Violet, Izella, Shahin, and Edith were in Berrien Springs. I longed to be with them, but somehow it seemed right that I should be in California. I cannot tell you why. I believe with all my heart that God directed me here. I can't wait to find out what He has in mind...Aunt Despina, cousin Dorothy and Howard met me at the airport and have helped me ever since. We made quite a foursome getting me registered at La Sierra

College...I'm living in the dormitory and have a nice roommate...I'm getting new glasses...Aunt Despina, Howard, and Dorothy look the same, but Aunt Alexandra seems to have aged a lot. Even with the mechanical devise, her hearing is poor.'" And the First Epistle of Indra to Lebanon went on.

Other letters followed giving the parents vivid accounts of what was happening in their daughter's life. One read, "I have often wondered why God brought me here, stripped away from my Middle East friends at EMC. Then I read this passage from Ellen White which seemed to be written especially for me:

> Your only safety and happiness are in making Christ your constant Counselor. You can be happy in Him if you had not another friend in the world. Your feelings of unrest, of homesickness, or loneli-ness may be for your own good. Your heavenly Father means to teach you to find in Him the friend-ship and love and consolation that will satisfy your most earnest hopes and desires...Find time to comfort some other heart, to bless with a kind, cheering word...(Letter 2 b, 1874).

"I can clearly see that I would never have felt my need of Him so much if I had been in Berrien with my friends. I still think about them, though, and the good times I'm missing. I'd surely like to get in on one of Shahin's fun parties again."

Indra wrote about her classes, work, and new friends. "I have many friends here now. The day I registered I met Lee Greer who seems to be a most devoted Christian. He is a graduate of the University of Texas with a degree in entomology. He was working in a research laboratory when he learned and accepted the Adventist message. His family are still strict Baptists and are not reconciled with his becoming a Seventh-day Adventist. Lee gave up a good job in Texas and came out here to study effective methods in soul winning."

In February La Sierra College held an evangelistic campaign. Indra and Lee got involved in the project and thoroughly enjoyed working together for souls.

"I am impressed with Lee's Christian courtesy and his love for Jesus and others. He respects me a great deal for my ideals," Indra's next letter read.

"Diamondola, do you detect the first signs of love developing between our daughter and the young man, Lee?" Aram asked.

"Yes," she responded. "I hope Indra keeps her feet on the ground and us completely informed."

By springtime every letter from Indra included news about Lee. "Lee will canvass in the Norfolk, Nebraska, area this summer. The church pastor has asked Lee to assist him with the four churches in his district. Lee asked them if I could canvass there this summer, also."

"How noble of Lee to get Indra a job near him," quipped Aram. "Sounds serious now. I think I hear wedding bells in our daughter's future."

"Oh, don't be presumptuous, Aram. Maybe Lee just wanted to make sure Indra had work that would assure her of a colporteur scholarship for next winter."

"Don't be so naive, my Dear," Aram scoffed. He didn't buy Diamondola's reasoning. "A father can read the handwriting, even if you can't."

At the close of the school year Indra flew to Omaha where Elder and Mrs. Page met her and took her to their home in Lincoln, Nebraska. She and Lillian Anderson canvassed the Fremont area while Lee and Carl worked in Norfolk. Indra wrote to her parents describing many of her interesting colporteur experiences. But always there was something special in the letter about Lee. "We both love canvassing. On Sabbaths Lee preaches in two different churches, and then he drops by to visit us. Elder Page tells me that Lee is highly intelligent and preaches as if he'd been in ministerial work all his life…"

"Will you believe me now?" Aram asked Diamondola. "We are reading more about Lee and his successes than about Indra and hers. I'm going to write and ask her plainly just what is going on between them. I want to know if he admires her as much as she does him, and if she plans to marry him?"

"ARAM! Sometimes you're as tactless as a hornet. Indra will tell us when, and if, she has definite plans."

But Aram wrote anyway, asking Indra for details.

July 24 he got this reply: "Daddy Dearest, I don't know how to answer your question about Lee. HE comes to see ME as often as he can spare the time, showering me with attention. He constantly reminds me that we have much in common—biology, nature, soul winning, etc. Does it not seem to you that Lee is hinting at a serious relationship?"

"It surely does!" Aram commented, slightly amused. "As a man, I recognize Lee's courting pattern. He leads a woman gently along until she realizes she wants to marry him. Then he asks her."

"Is that what you did?" Diamondola teased.

"That's what I tried, but you were harder to convince than the average girl. I deserved my prize when I got you. No one ever had to work as hard…"

"Except Jacob," Diamondola finished Aram's sentence.

July 31, Indra wrote: "Please continue to pray that God will lead us. Lee talks freely of his strong love for me, and I find more to admire in him daily. We are discussing the possibility of getting married. I wish you were here to counsel with me. I do rely upon God for impressions, but sometimes I wish I could hear Him talk directly."

August 13th's letter revealed what the parents knew was coming all the time. "Lee and I have been praying much about our future. It appears it is God's will that we marry. Lee is going to write to you. Please take time to pray about it before you answer him. I want to be sure I'm doing the right thing."

162

Then came the formal letter from Lee asking for Indra's hand in marriage:

"Dear Mr. and Mrs. A. E. Ashod, During the past 10 months I have come to know and love your daughter, Indra. We have gone to school together and are now in the Lord's work together. We share the same interests and goals. After considerable thought and prayer, we concluded that it is God's will for us to unite our efforts and lives through marriage. Before proceeding with further plans, I desire your consent to take Indra for my wife. Whatever is your decision in this matter, I will respectfully abide with it. I look forward to hearing from you soon. Sincerely, Lee Greer."

The Ashods did pray about Indra and Lee's possible marriage. They had already been praying about it for sometime—ever since Lee became a notable theme in Indra's letters. They had known then what their answer would be. The young man was quality Christian, ambitious and intelligent. Ashods knew Indra wouldn't look for anything less in a prospective spouse. They believed God had led Indra to California to meet Lee. Since it seemed to be God's doings, they wrote their approval.

The dawn of Indra's wedding day, September 9, 1962, burst bright and promising over the Nebraska prairies. Unlike most brides, Indra felt a twinge of sadness tear at her heart. This was the most important day in her life, and the two dearest people on earth to her would not be there to share her joy. Having to borrow a wedding dress did not bother her, but having to borrow "parents"—? Since neither set of parents were present, the Pages filled the void. The couple appreciated their effort, but they were still substitutes. Meanwhile, back in Lebanon, two teary-eyed parents spent the day imagining the scene in Nebraska and celebrating in spirit the high point in Indra's life.

Indra wore a floor-length gown of lace over net and satin and a finger-tip veil. Carol Page was the maid of honor, and the best man was Carl Hill, Lee's canvassing partner and mentor. (It was Carl who taught Lee the message three years earlier when they served together in the army.) The minister, Elder Page, made the service special and personal. Friends recorded the event for the Ashods on audio tape and on film.

Like the wedding ceremony, the reception was also held in Pages' home. Indra cut the wedding cake with a Jezzine knife, a gazelle-horn type of cutlery made only in Jezzine, Lebanon. Other reminders of Indra's past was the presence of friends from the Middle East—former neighbor David Rice and ex-missionaries families, the Gordon Zytkoskees and the Cecil Gemmells.

Indra and Lee went right to their new work, which was really an extension of what Lee had been doing all summer. Lee continued his colporteur work in Norfolk and helped Elder Heitzman in the ministry. The two men took turns preaching in the four district churches.

Back in Lebanon, the Ashods followed the Middle East custom of having a reception for their daughter in absentia. Alice Fund and the author made a huge wedding cake; the Ashods prepared other wedding treats. Wayne Olson emceed a program that consisted of playing the wedding tape and displaying the pictures from Nebraska. The many friends who gathered on the college campus lawn made an audio tape for the newly-weds, sending Lee their congratulations and Indra their love. Certainly Indra would have to translate to Lee the messages given in six different languages. The multi-lingual tape from friends in Lebanon became a treasured keepsake for Indra and Lee.

Indra wrote faithfully to her lonely parents. At Christmas she wrote, "I was happy that we would spend Christmas with Lee's family in Texas but was quite nervous about meeting them. When we arrived, his mother welcomed us with tears of joy. Soon his father came home, and he too welcomed us. They apologized to Lee for giving him trouble when he became a Seventh-day Adventist. I can understand why Lee's departure from their faith caused them concern—they are a Christian, closely-knit family.* They originated in Ireland but immigrated to Mississippi. I love to listen to their combination of a southern drawl and Irish brogue; they enjoy my Turkish English accent. Lee's sister, parents, aunts, uncles, and cousins are all lovely and loving people. When it came time to leave them, we all wept. Up until this time I had never met any of Lee's family, and he still hasn't met any of mine. Now he thinks it is time that he meets you. He invites you to come and live near us. Since you are retiring next month, you no longer have anything to hold you there in Lebanon. Lee says to start working on your papers immediately."

Diamondola sank to the settee and caught her breath. "Oh, I would really like to do that, Aram. Despina, like Joseph, has been trying to bring all of her family into her Egypt—the United States. She succeeded in getting everyone there except us. Do you think it would be possible for Indra and Lee to get us there?"

"Don't ever underestimate the Lord. He's pulled us over many mountains of difficulty. Just look what He did for Indra in one year's time. She went to America for an education and got the bonus of a Christian husband. Who knows, maybe retirement will bring a bonus for us."

*Eventually, some of Lee's family became Seventh-day Adventists.

Chapter 29

LAYING DOWN THE MANTLE

Moses asked a favor of God: "Let me go over and see the good land beyond the Jordan—that fine hill country and LEBANON." Deuteronomy 3:25

While Moses had asked to SEE Lebanon, Ashods were wanting to LEAVE Lebanon, and "go over and see the good land beyond the ocean—America!" All of their family now lived in America—Diamondola's sisters and their families, and Indra and Lee. Alexandra and Susanna were now in their eighties and were becoming quite feeble. Diamondola especially wanted to spend a little time with them. Now that Aram was officially retired, there was nothing to keep God's ambassadors in the Middle East any longer. So Despina in California and the Ashods in Lebanon combined their efforts to secure U.S. emigration papers for Diamondola and Aram. Unfortunately, they seemed to be making little progress.

"I just don't understand why our plans are stagnated like this," Diamondola complained. "We have sacrificed a life-time of opportunities to be with family in order to serve the Lord. Now we are old, and we need their support. Despina has guaranteed to care for us in America, so we won't be a financial burden to the U.S. government. Why the hold up? I wish God would grant us this desire of my heart, but I'm getting discouraged."

"Now, my Dear, don't blame God. He's taken us over many hurdles, but He does it in His good time. We'll wait patiently. Don't be discouraged."

But it was discouraging. As the winter of 1962–63 dragged by, they seemed no nearer their goal than they had been the previous autumn. They spent months trying to get police records from each country in which they had lived, verifying that Ashods had clean slates. Turkey and Iran never acknowledged their requests. They had the Lebanese records, but they would soon be out-dated. The United States would accept no police records that were more than three months old. Frustration set in. It seemed these three disinterested countries would never deliver police records that were current enough to issue visas to America. Diamondola's delicate stomach threatened to entertain a case of ulcers.

To give Ashods relief from this stress, Dr. Garo (a convert of Tcharakian from the deportation march) suggested they go with him for a day's outing to Biblical Tyre on the seashore. Ashods welcomed the invitation. The next morning Dr. Garo, two friends, and the Ashods were on their way. After they had driven for sometime, Dr. Garo parked the car so they could get out and stretch their legs. Diamondola felt sleepy, so she decided to stay in the car and take a nap while the others explored the beach. Aram left with the group but then decided to go back and check on Diamondola. For some reason, he did not see a car approaching as he crossed the road. The car hit him head on. Aram was airborne and landed on the hood of the car. When the terrorized driver stopped, Aram slid gently to the ground, landing on his feet. Aram's friends stood transfixed, watching the whole ordeal. It appeared to them that Aram was miraculously lifted onto the hood of the car. Other than a few bruises, Aram was unscathed.

"Only God knows what really happened," Aram said, still a little shaken. "I'm glad He was watching out for me—obviously I wasn't."

The two small bruises on Aram's back disappeared within a few days, and he was back working on their emigration papers. Iran finally sent a letter indicating that their police records in Iran were clear, but by then their Lebanese records were outdated. With these irregular documents and none from Turkey, they decided to appeal to the magnanimity of the vice consul at the American Embassy. They had dealt with him before, and he had been encouraging and friendly. His secretary, however, greeted them indifferently, "You don't have your documents in order." A fact they realized. "It is, therefore, futile for you to wait for the vice consul."

"We will wait," Aram said firmly but courteously.

They waited patiently for two hours, but still they were not invited into the vice consul's office. The Ashods' omnipresence became disconcerting to the secretary. She finally called in to the vice consul (who had probably been there all the time) asking, "What shall I do with this sweet old couple? I think they intend to become permanent fixtures." Pause. "Send them in? Good!"

During the next few minutes the consul scrutinized Ashods' incomplete records. Then he called the secretary, "Give them visas to the U.S."

"But," she argued, "they don't have their Turkish police records, and the Lebanese records..."

"Oh, never mind particulars," the vice consul snapped. "These folks won't threaten the security of the U.S. nor be a financial burden—her sister guarantees them. Give them their visas right away."

The next hour was a blur—a beautiful, unbelievable dream for Diamondola and Aram. They were still in euphoria when they left the American Embassy with their visas and papers all in order. Did they remember to thank the Consul? Kiss the secretary's hand? Kneel and pray? They couldn't recall. But there weren't enough positive superlatives in the English language to describe their elation as they returned home that night.

During the next few days, Olsons helped Ashods crate and label the goods they wanted shipped to the U.S. The rest of their things they sold or gave away. A huge farewell party for the Ashods was held at the Division Compound. The next day Diamondola and Aram were escorted to the airport by scores of well-wishers. Just before they entered the security area, Aram took off the helmet he had worn for years in the Middle East and placed it on Wayne Olson's head. "Like Elijah's mantle, I pass my ambassadorial work on to you, Wayne, as ministerial secretary for the division, and you must pass it on to the younger workers. Men, wear it devotedly."

This symbolic act brought on a flood of tears among the mission group. Although everyone was happy that Ashods would go to their family where they could enjoy a few years of leisure and peace, yet it was with sadness that the crowd bid farewell to God's faithful ambassadors who had been an inspiration to others in the Middle East for 45 years.

Chapter 30

GOLDEN DAYS

Indra and Lee left early to meet the Ashods at the airport in Omaha. Indra paced excitedly in the lobby, waiting for Diamondola and Aram to get their immigration papers processed. When they finally emerged from the security room, she flew into their arms. Hugs, kisses, and tears communicated the words that couldn't get past the lumps in their throats during the first few minutes.

"Your dear faces are the most beautiful ones in the world," Indra cried as she hugged both parents at once. "I thought you'd never get here."

"And we thought we'd never see you again," Diamondola said as she mopped the moisture from her eyes and nose. More hugs and kisses.

Lee cleared his throat.

"Oh, yes, this is Lee." Indra finally remembered to introduce her husband who had been quietly waiting and watching the emotional reunion. The next few hours were a blur of excited chatter and orientation. Lee was all that Ashods had expected and more. His gentle, caring nature immediately endeared him to them, and Lee adopted Ashods as his second parents.

"September is such a special month for our family," Indra observed. "Do you realize nearly everything good happens to us in September—you were married September 21, and we were

170

married September 9. I came to the states on September 14 two years ago; now you arrive September 3. AND I met Lee in September."

Ashods spent three wonderful months with Lee and Indra; then the harsh Nebraska winters drove them to seek the sunny climes of southern California. Diamondola spent the Christmas of 1963 with her three sisters. It was the first holiday they had been together in almost 60 years. During the next few months Despina, Diamondola, Susanna, and Alexandra basked together in the California sun recalling their happy, though austere, childhood. They recounted their extraordinary life experiences and blessed the God who had seen them through wars, separation, and devastating times.

Alexandra (86) and Susanna (84) had become very feeble; both died during the summer of 1964. The parting, however, was very difficult for Diamondola and Despina. After all the years of separation, they had been reunited only a few months. The golden days of their golden years had been far too few.

The arrival of Indra and Lee in Loma Linda during the same summer brought back the joy of living. This blessing was due to Lee's decision to study physical therapy at Loma Linda Medical Center. Baby Lee was an extra bonus. Immediately he became the center of their lives.

"I declare there is nothing like a new life to spark life," Diamondola smiled as she played peek-a-boo with the baby on her lap.

"It's my turn now, Diamondola," Aram said as he lifted the baby onto his knee. He bounced little Lee up and down and sang Armenian songs. The child laughed and cooed, and Aram's heart beat with pleasure.

"You're just a doting old grandfather, Aram," Diamondola teased.

"And loving every minute of it," Aram admitted. "Between the two of us we should be able to spoil him pretty good."

Time passed quickly. In March of 1966 granddaughter Ruth arrived. Lee graduated from the physical therapy course that spring and began working at the hospital. The Greer and Ashod families were both settled comfortably in little bungalows.

"What a perfect retirement set-up we have. We enjoy Indra and Lee and have the fun of watching the grandchildren grow and develop," Aram said.

"How true! Have you noticed how many words little Lee is saying?" Diamondola asked.

"Yes, I have. Not that I can understand him, but his chatter is music to this old man's ears. And little Ruth is just as dear."

During the next two years Aram completed translating *Desire of Ages* into Armenian. So devoted was he to the task, his last contribution to the Middle East, he nearly lost his eyesight. From that time on his vision was impaired.

In 1968 Gordon Zytkoskee, personnel manager at the new Kettering Hospital in Dayton, Ohio, persuaded Lee to join their staff in the physical therapy department. When the Greers moved, the Ashods followed.

Two happy years in Kettering passed quickly, and then the Advent movement reached out its arm again. The General Conference called Lee to replace Jack Thompson in the clinic in Teheran, Iran. Dr. Arzoo, who remembered Ashods' little Indra, was responsible for the call. The Ashods were happy to loan their daughter and family to work in the Middle East. Indra had spent five happy years of her childhood in Iran. Plans were laid for everyone, including Diamondola and Aram, to leave for the land of Esther. They passed their physicals and got their passports, visas, and immunizations. The six were all set to go to Iran.

Then a good friend of Ashods, Mrs. Eileen Drousault, who had been the librarian at Loma Linda University but had since moved to take the same position in Southern Missionary College, phoned. "I've been thinking that it might not be the best idea for you two to go to Iran with Indra and Lee. I've found a nice little two-bedroom house with reasonable rent here in Collegedale. I will be nearby and can keep an eye on you. Pray about it and let me know."

"Now if that isn't switching trains before leaving the station," Aram objected. "I'm anxious to see our old friends in Iran and contribute what I can to the work there." But after careful thought and much prayer, Ashods decided that it would probably be better for them to stay at Collegedale.

Separating from the grandchildren was almost more than Diamondola could bear. The first few weeks she cried and regretted that she had not gone with them. But Ashods weren't lonely for long. Eileen introduced some college students to them. Soon the Ashods' house became a Sabbath afternoon retreat for students and community friends who never tired of hearing the Ashods' exploits in the Middle East. (Some of her experiences are told in the book *Diamondola*.) Diamondola further extended her Abrahamic hospitality by serving delectable Middle East cuisine to her guests. They always came back for more.

One quiet evening after supper the Ashods were alone in their house, talking about the "children in Iran", when the doorbell rang. Aram opened the door; a young man and his pregnant wife pushed their way in. They were dressed rather shabbily and were very much out of breath.

"We're Pete and Rita. Our car broke down, and we've been walking a long time. We're exhausted and hungry," the young man panted.

Diamondola was touched with their hard luck story and decided to help them. "You two just sit down and talk with Aram, while I get you some victuals."

Diamondola's heart swelled with pleasure as she warmed the left over rice and vegetables. "Some have entertained angels unawares," she said to herself. "Perhaps this is my turn. God's just fooling me a little by sending me His most unkempt, ah, angels."

In a few minutes Diamondola had a substantial meal on the table, and the strangers ate heartily and hurriedly. "We hate to eat and run," the man said rising from the table, "but we've got to go. Thanks a lot." Then the two disappeared into the blackness of the night.

Diamondola sang as she cleared the table and prepared for bed. Her spirits were soaring; she had helped someone who was really down and out. Her quiet reverie was abruptly interrupted by the doorbell's frantic jangle followed by a loud knock.

"Let us in. We're the police."

Startled out of her senses, Diamondola slipped on her house-coat and ran barefooted to the door. The police brushed past her and looked about the house as they bombarded her with questions. "Where is that man and woman who were just here? What did they do? What did they want?"

"Wh-why, I don't know. They were hungry, and I fed them," Diamondola stammered.

"FED THEM!?!?" the officer exploded. Shaking his head in disbelief, he turned to his companion. "Criminals wanted in three states, and she FED them!"

The police backed out the door, staring incredulously at little Diamondola.

"Well," Diamondola exhaled explosively, "so much for the 'angels' I entertained. Aram, do you suppose the police will get me for aiding and abetting criminals?"

"No," Aram said taking a deep breath, "but hopefully our kind deed and what we said will make them want to turn their life around. I prayed with them too."

Letters arriving from Iran—otherwise known as the Second Epistles of Indra—always made that day special. "Lee has been very busy at the clinic which is only down the hall from our apart-ment. The children and I find excuses to go there often since they have air conditioning…. Lee has picked up a lot of the Farsee language and I'm re-learning mine.

174

"I feel so enveloped in the middle of this large city. The high walls around the compound ought to give me a sense of security, but they don't. A number of children have been kidnapped, so I never let mine out of my sight. I'm glad we've got Atlas, our Iranian sheep dog. He's loyal to us but tolerates no strangers.

"Sometimes we go out to the Iran Training School in Shimran to see Johnny and Angel (Dikran) Minassian. We enjoy the country atmosphere while eating a potluck dinner together. One of the students is a relative of the Shah. He plays with the children. IMAGINE THAT—your grandkids associate with royalty!.

"I'm having a wonderful time getting re-acquainted with friends from my childhood days. The sons and daughters of the workers with whom you associated are now the workers with whom we associate."

Aram and Diamondola reached back into their memories. They had gone to Iran in 1931 and this was now 1971. Had it been 40 years? Time had slipped by softly on feathered wings.

September 21, 1971, a very important day in the lives of the Ashods, arrived. It was time to celebrate 50 years of marriage. Aram was now 87 and Diamondola 77. As usual, when Ashods had a big occasion to celebrate, there were no family members present to share in the event.

But Lee and Indra had remembered the day by preparing an appropriate gift. On the day of Ashods' anniversary a student from Iran arrived at SMC bringing with him a card and a very special gift from Indra and Lee.

"What a wonderful way to begin the day marking the half century we have spent together," Aram said as he kissed his little Diamond.

"That's right. Even if the kids can't be here, they remembered. Although we are alone on this special day, far from family and old friends, just being alive and together is a blessing," Diamondola sighed contentedly.

But they weren't alone for long. Soon friends from the community and college began to pour in. Throughout the day, well-wishers arrived at about 15 minute intervals. They brought flowers, cards, candy, and golden gifts. Ashods suspected that Eileen had orchestrated this super, stupendous, marvelous day, and they were grateful to those who made their golden wedding anniversary a memorable occasion.

Chapter 31

JUST RESTING

Diamondola and Aram were excited. Indra and family were coming back to the States after a three-year mission stint in Iran. Lee had accepted employment in the Takoma Hospital in Greenville, Tennessee. Ashods would join them there; they would be together again.

The Ashods left their good friends at Collegedale but soon made new ones in Greenville. The next four years with Indra, Lee, and the grandchildren were happy ones. Ashods' life quickly settled into a routine—daily walks, volunteer work at the church or hospital, and play with Lee III and Ruth.

"I'm not just a proud grandfather when I say those children are real scholars and devoted little Christians. They are!"

"And, don't forget, nice looking too," Diamondola laughed.

"I hope they will contribute in some way to further the kingdom of God," Aram said wistfully. "I wish I could live to see them in their life's work."

"Don't talk like that, Aram. Jesus may come before they grow up."

On the night of August 9, 1977, Nancy Krohn, the lady in charge of medical records at the Takoma Hospital, visited Ashods. She left shortly before 9 p.m. Then, as usual, Ashods had worship together and prepared for bed. Diamondola slept in a separate bedroom. She liked to read to fall asleep, and the light

177

kept Aram awake. He kissed her goodnight and went to his bedroom. Five minutes later he called to her, "Diamondola, please come in here. I just want to kiss you one more time before I go to sleep."

She went into his bedroom, they kissed tenderly, and said goodnight again. How could Diamondola know it would be goodnight forever? The next morning when Aram was not astir as usual, Diamondola went into his bedroom. As she leaned over his bed to call him, she noticed that he laid very still with a serene expression on his face. Instinctively, she knew he was dead. He had slipped away quietly sometime during the night. Did he suspect this was going to happen? Is that why he called her in for a last goodnight/goodbye kiss?

Although Diamondola knew Aram was just resting until the resurrection, the separation was most painful. Many times during the course of his service in the Middle East, Aram had faced dangers that could have ended his life violently. God had extended his years, however, and allowed Aram to die peacefully. Aram, ambassador for Jesus, was now awaiting the next directive from his Chief of State. This time he would be called into a perfect country that held no problematic working conditions.

Arrangements were made for him to be buried in Deacon's Cemetery in Wildwood, Georgia. *The Adventist Review*, the denomination's weekly paper, carried this brief account: Aram Ashod, born March 17, 1883, died August 9, 1977, at the age of 93 1/2 years. He leaves his wife Diamondola, daughter Indra, son-in-law Lee Greer, and grandchildren, Lee III and Ruth. He worked 45 years for the denomination as secretary, treasurer, evangelist, mission president, translator, and editor in four countries of the Middle East—Turkey, Iran, Cyprus, and Lebanon.

Diamondola, Aram's co-ambassador, missed her companion of 56 years almost more than she had imagined possible. Right after Aram's demise, she moved with Lee and Indra to

Wildwood, Georgia. The new location helped to block out the memories she and Aram shared of Greenville. Two years later they all moved on to Jellico, Tennessee. Then, in 1981 Lee received a call from the General Conference to work in the physical therapy department of the Masanga Leprosy Hospital in Sierra Leone, West Africa.

"What shall we do with mother?" Indra questioned. "She is 87 now, and I'm afraid to take her with us since I'm not acquainted with living conditions there. I can't just leave her here alone, either. Perhaps we shouldn't go, Lee."

When Diamondola learned of their dilemma, she encouraged them by saying, "This is a call from God. Of course you must go. I will miss you during the two years you'll be gone, but we won't be separated forever. If I should die before you return, we'll just plan to meet again in heaven. In the meantime, I'll find someone with whom I may live."

Arrangements were made for Diamondola to live with Bedour Farag (Wadie's sister) and her husband Wadi Awad, friends from the Middle East now living in Collegedale. Diamondola couldn't choke back the tears as she bade goodby to Indra and family. Almost before Indra left the States, a mantle of heaviness settled upon her. Collegedale wasn't the same after her absence of eight years; no one could ease the pain Diamondola sometimes felt as she remembered happier days there with Aram, Eileen, and the caring college students and friends. Because of her despondency, Diamondola's delicate stomach became more sensitive. Bedour lovingly fixed special food to alleviate her health problem, but the medicine Diamondola needed most was in Africa. This the Awads could not give her—no surrogate family could replace her real children at this stage in her life.

Oh, there were happy days for Diamondola too. The Awads invited in guests that Diamondola would enjoy. Old friends from the Middle East dropped by when they were in town. Occasionally, she saw Despina and family who had moved to North Carolina, only 400 miles away. But with Aram gone and

Indra in Africa, there was still a big void in Diamondola's life. She hoped she would live to see Indra and family again. She counted the days until their return.

During the summer of 1983, Diamondola's wish was fulfilled. The Greers came home on furlough and, once again, she held her loved ones in her arms. New life surged through Diamondola's frail little body. She determined never to be separated from them in this life again—no matter what.

The five of them went to Texas to see Lee's family. Then they were off to Berrien Springs, Michigan, for the month-long, inspiring Mission Institute. While there the Greers and Diamondola saw Elly Economou, Shahin, Edith, the Olsons, the Russells, and many other friends from the Middle East. Diamondola's health improved, and, surrounded by family, she felt whole again.

When the Greers' furlough time was up, Diamondola had her passport and papers ready to go to Africa with them. She was more excited than the children. "Do you know that this trip fulfills the head teacher's prophecy made at my high school graduation? She said, 'Diamondola will be a missionary in Africa and other places.' But I'll bet she never thought I would be 89 before it happened."

Diamondola sat so small in her British Caledonia airplane seat that she was almost lost from view, but the Little Dynamite was fired with excitement. She hopped up once in awhile to catch the view from the plane's window as they flew south from London over France, Spain, and Africa. "Oh, look at the green forests along the Atlantic coast of Africa! Just think, we'll soon be in Africa where Livingstone left his heart." Her excitement was contagious, even for the Greers who had enjoyed the same sight only three months earlier.

When they landed at Sierra Leone, Diamondola popped out of the plane as soon as the doors were opened. "Oh, look at those handsome black men! The women are straight as hickory sticks and so graceful. Aren't those babies darling? Oh, I know I'm just going to enjoy every minute here. Whee! It is rather hot, isn't it?" Diamondola continued a running commentary on the sights and sounds of Africa that scintillated her senses.

Lee cleared their belongings through customs, while Indra tried to curb her mother's enthusiasm/excitement. The next few hours were a blur of wonderment to Diamondola. Later she recalled that they had been entertained by Joseph Allen, the mission president. She definitely remembered the long, dusty, bumpy ride to the Masanga Leprosy Hospital and the royal welcome the Greers received at the mission compound. Everyone was hugging everyone else. Diamondola engaged in the hugging activity too, even though she didn't know any of them yet. It just felt good to be hugged.

Her first sight of the leprosy patients repulsed Diamondola. The gnarled hands, deformed bodies, missing fingers, toes, ears, and noses drew large portions of pity from her loving heart. "God compares sin to leprosy," she thought. "How loathsome sin must be to Him. Even so, He loves the victims!"

Diamondola was immediately dubbed "old grandmummy" by the Africans who have great respect for old people. "Here it's a blessing to be old—it's nice to be special," Diamondola commented, more than a little pleased. "Those little pickins (African word for children), are special in my sight."

The Greers' house was about a mile up the hill from the mission complex which consisted of offices, physical therapy clinic, seven wards, and a church. Within a few days Diamondola ventured all the way down to the compound by herself. "And I made sure Lee saw me before I started back up the hill," she boasted to Indra. "I just want you all to know that Grandmummy can still step lively." No one had ever doubted it.

Diamondola soon felt a special burden for the African women. Often she observed a man walking down the road, swinging his empty arms leisurely, while his poor pregnant wife stumbled after him—a basket of bananas and oranges on her head, a baby slung on her back, and a little one hanging onto her skirts. Many times little Grandmummy went up to the tall African and reprimanded him. "That your wife?" she would ask the man.

"Yes, Grandmummy."

"Is she a good wife? Does she care for your children and your garden?" she prodded.

"Yes, Grandmummy," he answered politely looking down at the little woman who hardly came up to his armpits.

Then she shook her finger and solemnly advised him, "You must not make her do all the work. You must help her. You carry the tub of food and the baby. God wants you to care tenderly for you wife."

The man smiled respectfully, "I'll think about that, Mum."

"That's not good enough. Do it NOW." And Diamondola watched as the transfer was made from the relieved woman to the reluctant husband. Then Diamondola went on her way humming a tune. Whether she succeeded in making those African husbands reform permanently is rather doubtful; at least, she had tried.

On the mission compound lived missionaries from Sweden, Holland, England, the United States and Africa, but they mostly used the English language to communicate. Some Africans spoke Creole, a sort of pidgin English, while others spoke the Timneh language. As Diamondola walked down the road the women and children would smile at her and say, "Indiraay." Diamondola was pleased that everyone in Sierra Leone seemed to know her daughter, Indra. She would smile back and say, "Yes, Indiraay is my daughter." This always seemed to confuse them. Then she learned that "indiraay" was the proper morning greeting in the Timneh language. The afternoon greeting was "pee-are-ee". The answer to both was "seke"—whatever that meant. She learned the Timneh words for "I love you, and God loves you too." She used them as often as she could.

Gitte Jacobsen, the wife of the Danish business manager, and Diamondola often visited in the homes of the Africans. One day a man from a village came out to the road where the two ladies

182

were walking. He bowed to Diamondola and said in English, "Lady, please bless me in the name of Jesus Christ." Diamondola was reasonably astonished but, as he knelt before her, she put her hand on his head and prayed for him. He arose, thanked her, and disappeared into the jungle. She never saw him again but often thought about the man that made her feel like the Biblical King Melchizedek giving Abraham his blessings.

Diamondola loved her walks in the woods. She declared that the African butterflies were the most beautiful in the world. The uniquely colored flowers and birds constantly fascinated her too. She did not have the same admiration for the snakes or the monkeys. She planned not to trespass on their territory, and hoped they would respect hers. She remembered the renegade monkey the Osters had kept in Teheran when Indra was a child.

The driver ants! Diamondola knew THEY were a creation of the devil! They had long pinchers, and on some strange cue, bit in unison in order to afflict the utmost pain on their victims. The driver ants follow the leader and walk in long black lines. If an innocent person, such as Diamondola, wanders along enjoying the scenery instead of keeping her/his eyes peeled to the ground and steps on the moving black line, then the "beasties" swarm all over their victim. The next step then is to stomp and slap at the ants while running for help to get someone to pick her/him clean of the creatures. Diamondola liked to go walking with Lee and Indra because they watched for the ants while she gazed about at her surroundings. When they yelled "ANTS!", they would grab her under the elbows and run with her. Her feet never touched the ground, but she propelled her legs just the same—maybe it would help just a little. When the danger was past, Lee and Indra would set Diamondola back on the ground, and her legs would then be on their own.

Sabbaths were special for Diamondola. Indra taught the junior Sabbath School class which had anywhere from 80 to 120 children. "Junior" meant anyone in the young bracket—baby to teen. Diamondola wrote to a friend, "How do you tell the story of the ten lepers to children to whom leprosy is a way of life? Yet they love all the Bible stories and those of Ellen White. It makes me want to cry to see all the misery, sickness, and deformity—yet the children have cheerful, smiling faces. Malnutrition is evident everywhere, and the 'old-man look' on the children's starving faces is all too common. When Indra asks the children how many of them have something for which they can thank God, almost every hand goes up. One boy said, 'I am thankful that God is giving me a good body.' He meant he was enjoying better health. He was still undernourished and deformed from polio, but he was in the middle of corrective surgeries. This meant he wouldn't have to crawl anymore, but could walk with calipers and crutches."

Communion services were especially meaningful in the leprosy hospital. First of all, feet really needed washing after they had trod the dusty African roads. Diamondola remembered that Jesus had touched the "uncleans"; so she washed the deformed feet of leprosy patients. Hands without fingers sometimes washed her feet. Then after the ceremony, Diamondola put her arms around her communion partner and squeezed her tight. One Sabbath she encouraged her blind partner by saying, "Someday God will restore us. He's got quite a bit of remodeling to do on both of us. Then we will be beautiful, and you will see me as I see you now. Won't that be a great day?"

Two years in Africa sped by too quickly, and it was time to return to the States to put Lee III and Ruth in college. Diamondola was sad as she closed the lid of her suitcase and rode to the Lungi Airport. The road was still dusty and bumpy. Half the time she was flying in the air as the jostle of the car tossed her about. Her active mind held many pleasant memories of her "missionary days" in Africa—a childhood dream fulfilled at last. At age 91 she knew she would never be back to this land of wonderful people.

Diamondola and the Greers stopped first in North Carolina to see Despina. After just a few days, Despina died (August 1985), but not before the sisters had time to re-affirm their faith that they would meet again after the brief "rest".

Back in the States, Lee, Indra, and Diamondola settled near the Kettering Memorial Hospital in Ohio. Lee III and Ruth left directly for Southwestern Adventist College in Texas.

Diamondola's last move was to Oklahoma with Lee and Indra in 1988. Time was taking its toll on God's fragile, aging ambassador. One day she told the author, "I, like Paul, have fought a good fight, I have finished my course, and now I'm waiting for the crown of righteousness. It's been marvelous, yet humbling, to serve as God's ambassador. My faith in Him is stronger than when I first embraced His love and accepted the commission to preach the gospel. Now I just want to rest from my labors until He awakens me for that extended holiday."

God released Diamondola from this life on May 12, 1990 at the age of 96 years. Now she is just resting until He calls her to the mansion He has prepared for Diamondola and Aram, His Middle East Ambassadors.

APPENDIX

AcMoody, C. D. — the American missionary with whom Diamondola made her first missionary journey into the heart of Turkey as his 13-year old translator.

Anthony, Theodore — the Greek shoemaker who immigrated to California, heard the Seventh-day Adventist message in his own language (a miracle because the sermons were given in English), accepted Adventism, and felt impressed to return to Turkey in February 1889 with the message. As he plied his cobbler's trade, he also preached the gospel.

Aresian, Ares — a young colporteur who became an Adventist minister. In 1913 he worked with Diamondola in Constantinople. They fell in love and were engaged in 1914. The mission sent him to Greece where he died of tuberculosis in 1916.

Ataturk, Kemal Mustafa — the Turkish hero of the Dardenelles who gradually took over control of Turkey after World War I. He instituted many reforms which were good; yet relations between the political and religious factions remained strained. (Ottoman Turks ruled the East Mediterranean countries from the 14th century until Ataturk).

Baharian, Zadour — Armenian convert of Anthony, baptized in 1890. He went to Basel, Switzerland where he studied for the ministry. In 1892 he returned to Turkey with literature he had translated and printed. Then he scattered it like the leaves of autumn. In 1893 he and Anthony held meetings in

Ovajuk, Bardizag, Aleppo, and Alexandretta. He was a fearless worker who was often arrested, beaten, and imprisoned. He was the first ordained, national minister in the Middle East (1894 by H. P. Holser). He brought the message to the Keanides family in Brousa. He died a martyr during World War I. (He was taken from prison, out of the city, and shot while praying).

Barlas, A. N. — one of two colporteurs that escaped the 1914–15 persecution of Christians. He continued to work in Turkey under adverse circumstances until he left for Cyprus in 1947. He contributed to the work there through the colporteur ministry and Bible work until his retirement.

Buzugerian, A. — Adventist worker who escaped to Egypt during the persecutions of World War I. He returned to the work in Turkey in 1920.

Derhousikian, Dikran — one of the two Armenian colporteurs who escaped execution in 1914–15. He fled to Beirut where Diamondola met him again in 1951.

Erzburgers — He was mission director in Turkey from 1917–1923, except when he was on furlough. During that period Ashods had to do all the work alone. Mrs. Erzburger was there when Diamondola was pronounced dead, and she helped prepare her body for burial (1919). Elder Erzburger married Diamondola and Aram in 1921.

Frauchiger, E. E — came as a mission director to Turkey in 1909. Diamondola made her third missionary visit into the heart of Turkey with him during the winter of 1915–16. They carried money, clothing, and food to relieve the suffering of the Adventists members who they found on the exile trail.

Gomig, Yebraxie — daughter of the first Turkish convert, Bible worker in Turkey, only national worker in Turkey from 1948–1959.

Greaves, Robert — missionary to Turkey, Greece, and Cyprus. He began the work in Smyrna, Turkey in 1907. Diamondola went on her second missionary journey with him in the spring of 1911 into Greece and Albania. He retired in Cyprus in 1932 to help establish the work there on a more permanent basis.

Larson, Aaron and Mrs. — good friends of Ashods who directed the first orphanage in Turkey in 1922.

Tcharakian, Diran — a University professor, famous author, and poet. When he became an Adventist, his family left him, and critics dubbed him crazy. He was the man of faith who, in the name of Jesus, resurrected Diamondola in 1919. He died on the exodus trail in 1920.

DIAMONDOLA'S FAMILY

Elijah — father

Theodora — mother

Alexandra (1879–1964), Susanna (1881–1964), and Despina (1895–1985) — sisters

Demitrius — uncle

Govreckian (Crisp), Nazareth — doctor who married Despina

Sava — Uncle

Xanthopoulas, Stavro — married Susanna. He died in Greece in 1937 of stroke.

Xanthopoulas, Pano — son of Susanna and Stavro

DIRECTORS/PRESIDENTS of the TURKISH MISSION/LEVANT UNION:

1890–1901 — under the Central European Mission & Central European Union

1901–1903 — Oriental Union Mission under European General Conference

1903–1906 — Dr. A. W. George in charge. Had a clinic in Constantinople with Alexandra Keanides as his assistant.

1907–1909 — C. D. AcMoody and Robert Greaves

1910–1916 — E. E. Frauchiger and A. Buzugherian

1917–1923 — some of the time Erzburger and Greaves. Sometimes Ashods were alone.

1924–1928 — M. C. Grin

1929–1934 — F. F. Backer

1934–1937 — Klinger

1938–1943 — F. F. Oster

1943–1948 — A. E. Ashod

1948–1952 — Ben Mondics (In 1951 the Turkish Mission came under the newly organized Middle East Division).

1952–1958 — Conrad Rasmussen (built the first Christian church in Turkey since 1917).

1958–2004 — I choose not to list all of these.

Theodor Anthony (left) was the Greek shoemaker who brought the Seventh-day Adventist message to Turkey in 1889. His first convert, Zadour Baharian (right), became the first ordained Seventh-day

Front row — Theodora Keanides, Elder Buzugerian, Elder & Mrs. Erzberger, Diamondola. Back row — Aram Ashod stands behind Erzberger.

Diran Tcharakian, poet, author, and university professor, became a
Seventh-day Adventist minister and was Turkey's modern Paul.

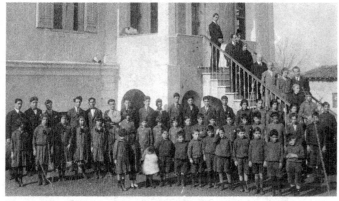

The orphanage Diamandola and Aram started later moved into the
basement of the Thessolonika Church in Greece in 1924.

At the Zee's estate in Larak, the Ashod family enjoyed picnics and quiet outings. From left, Aram, Indra, Grandma Theodora, and Diamondola.

Threshing grain at the Zee estate.

Diamondola, Aram and Indra.

A baptismal service at the Marmara Sea.

Diamondola, Aram, and Indra on their two-wheeled monsters in Cyprus.

Indra and Lee's wedding.

Aram and Diamondola with Lee III and Ruth.

We invite you to view the complete
selection of titles we publish at:

www.TEACHServices.com

or write or email us your praises,
reactions, or thoughts about this
or any other book we publish at:

TEACH Services, Inc.
P U B L I S H I N G
www.TEACHServices.com
P.O. Box 954
Ringgold, GA 30736

info@TEACHServices.com

TEACH Services, Inc., titles may be purchased in bulk for
educational, business, fund-raising, or sales promotional use. For
information, please e-mail

BulkSales@TEACHServices.com.

Finally, if you are interested in seeing
your own book in print, please contact us at

publishing@teachservices.com.

We would be happy to review your manuscript for free.

CPSIA information can be obtained
at www.ICGtesting.com
Printed in the USA
FSOW03n2356050218
44043FS